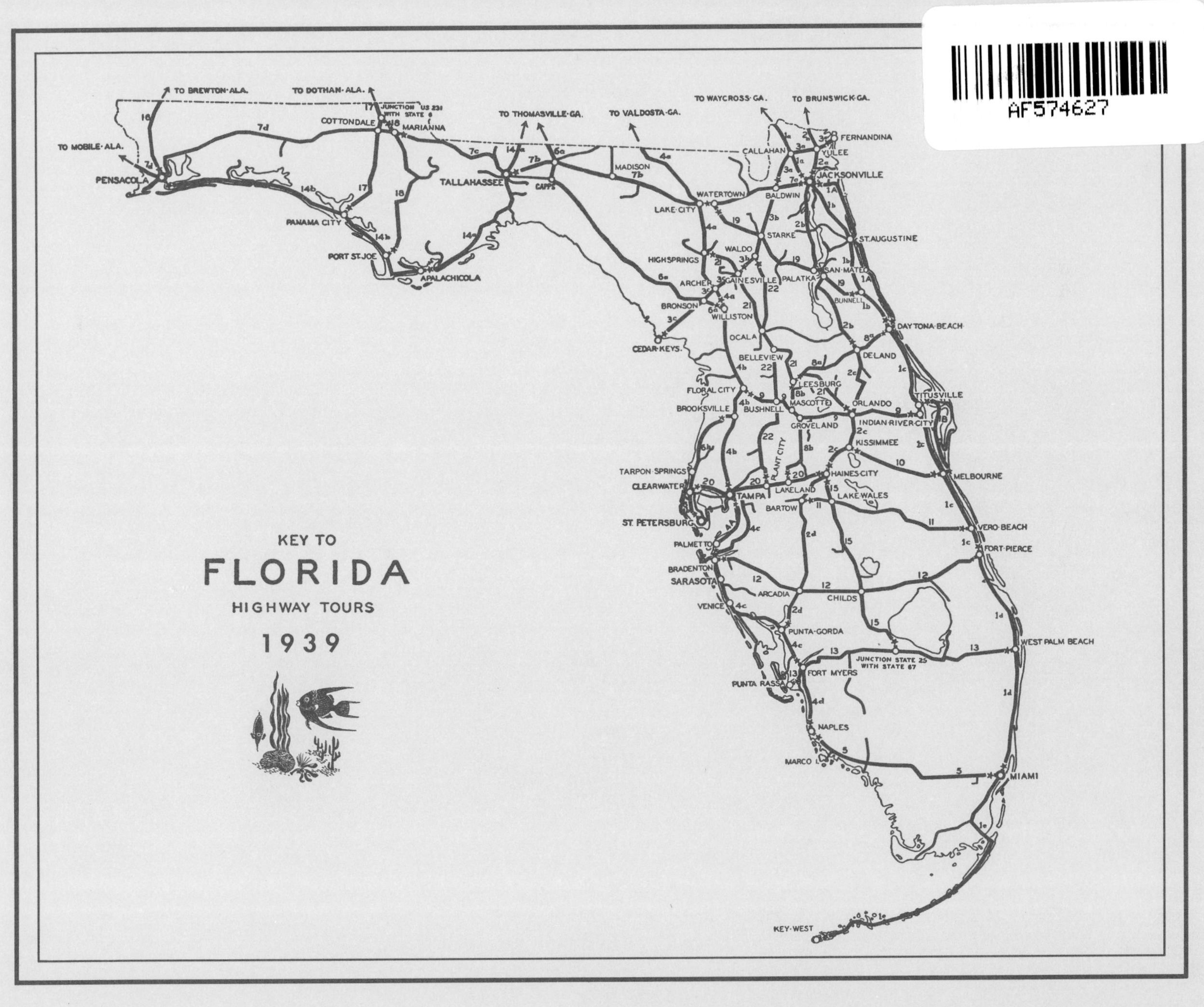

TO BREWTON·ALA.
TO DOTHAN·ALA.
JUNCTION US 231 WITH STATE 6
COTTONDALE
MARIANNA
TO THOMASVILLE·GA.
TO VALDOSTA·GA.
TO WAYCROSS·GA.
TO BRUNSWICK·GA.
FERNANDINA
CALLAHAN
YULEE
JACKSONVILLE
TO MOBILE·ALA.
PENSACOLA
TALLAHASSEE
CAPPS
MADISON
WATERTOWN
BALDWIN
LAKE·CITY
PANAMA CITY
PORT ST·JOE
APALACHICOLA
STARKE
ST.AUGUSTINE
HIGHSPRINGS
WALDO
PALATKA
SAN MATEO
ARCHER
GAINESVILLE
BUNNELL
BRONSON
WILLISTON
DAYTONA·BEACH
CEDAR·KEYS.
OCALA
DE·LAND
BELLEVIEW
LEESBURG
FLORAL CITY
TITUSVILLE
BROOKSVILLE
BUSHNELL
MASCOTTE
ORLANDO
GROVELAND
INDIAN·RIVER·CITY
KISSIMMEE
PLANT CITY
TARPON·SPRINGS
HAINES·CITY
MELBOURNE
CLEARWATER
TAMPA
LAKELAND
LAKE·WALES
BARTOW
ST. PETERSBURG
VERO·BEACH
KEY TO
FLORIDA
HIGHWAY TOURS
1939
PALMETTO
FORT·PIERCE
BRADENTON
SARASOTA
ARCADIA
CHILDS
VENICE
PUNTA·GORDA
WEST PALM BEACH
JUNCTION STATE 25 WITH STATE 67
FORT MYERS
PUNTA RASSA
NAPLES
MARCO
MIAMI
KEY·WEST

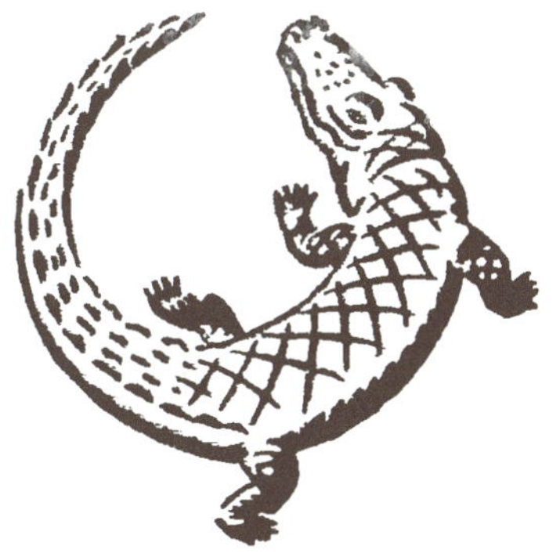

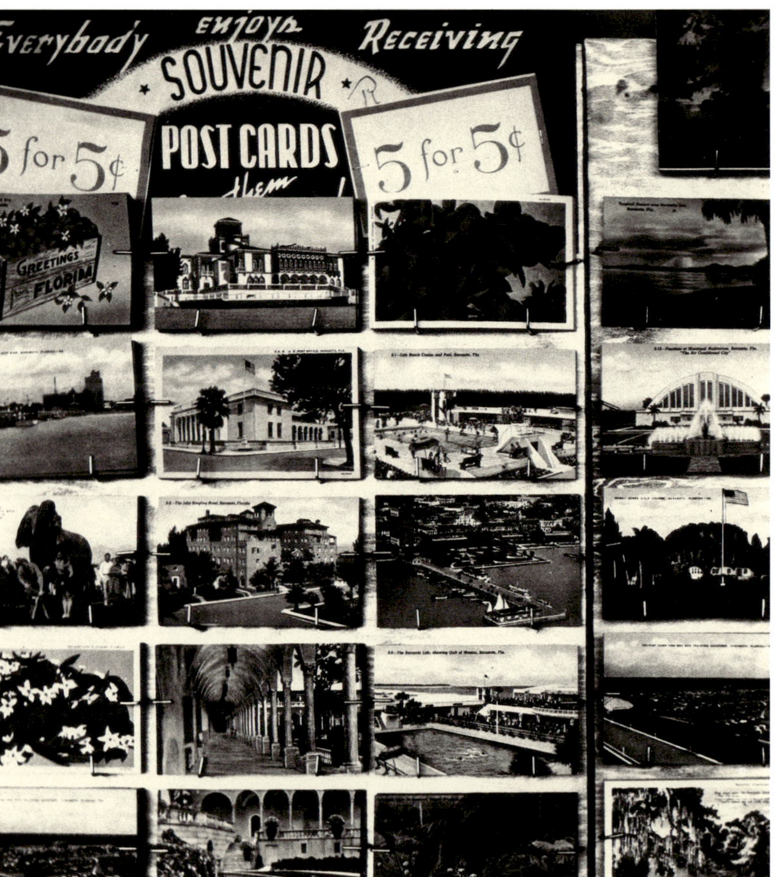

Everybody
enjoys
Receiving
SOUVENIR
POST CARDS
5 for 5¢
5 for 5¢
GREETINGS
FLORIDA

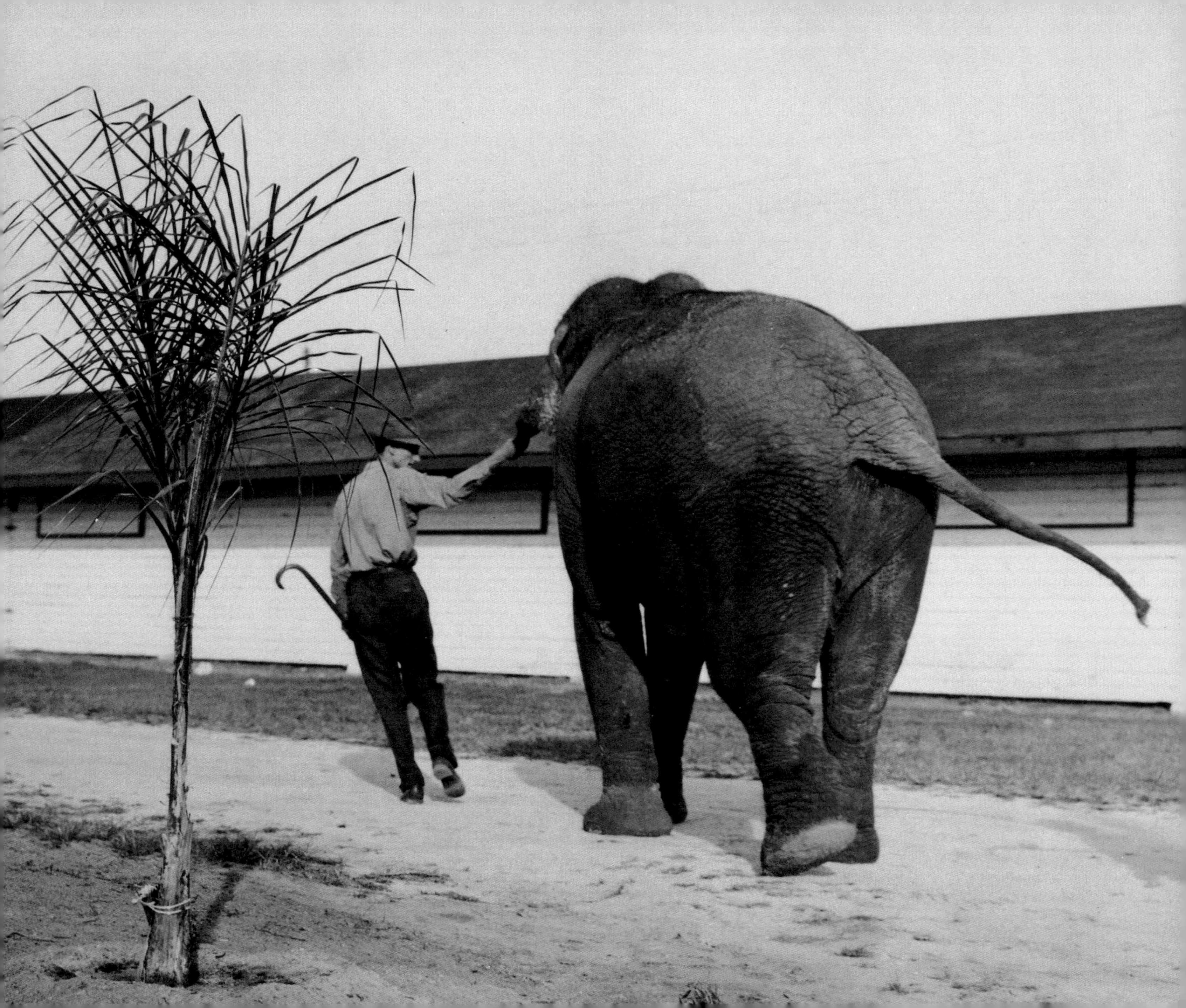

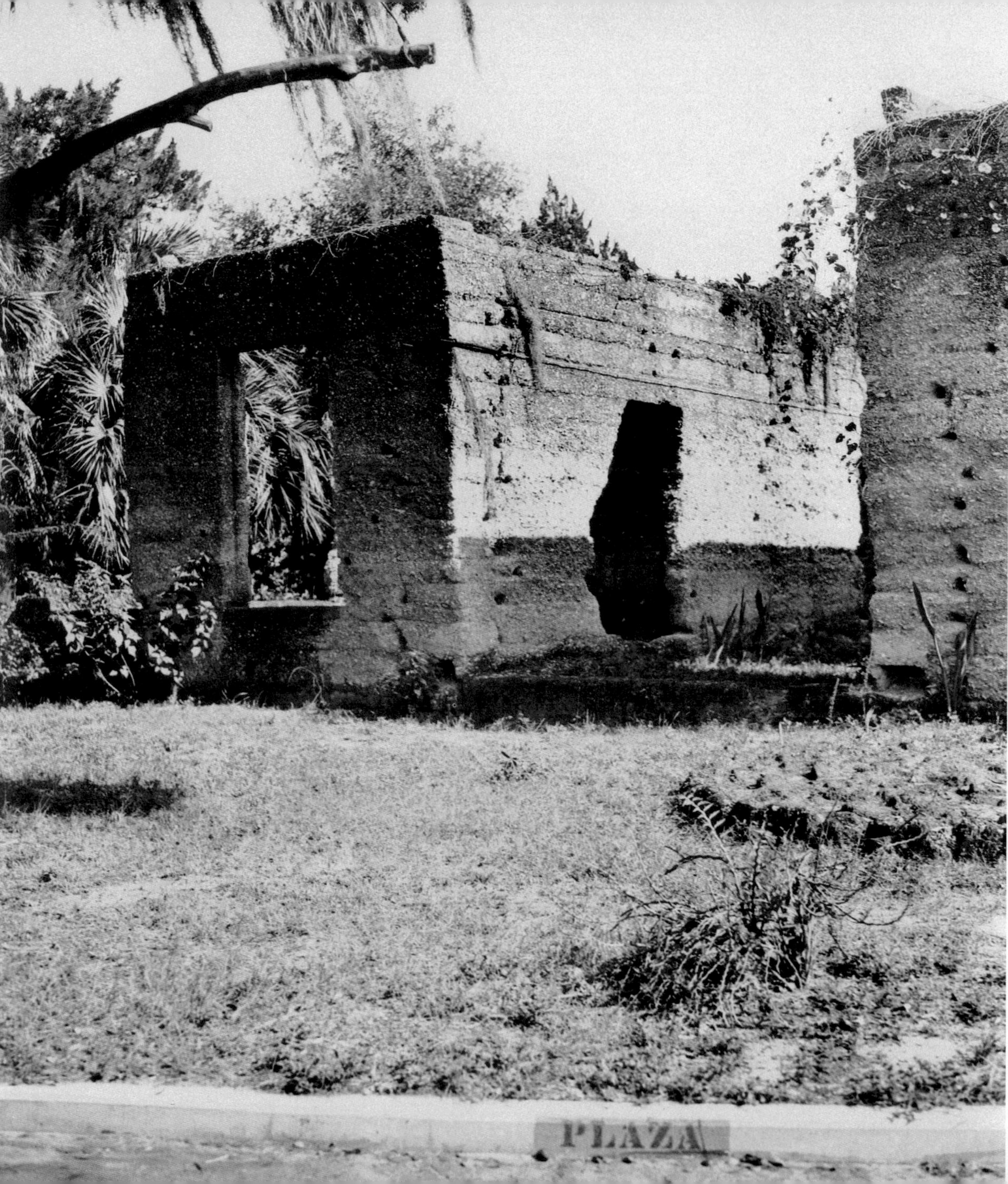
PLAZA

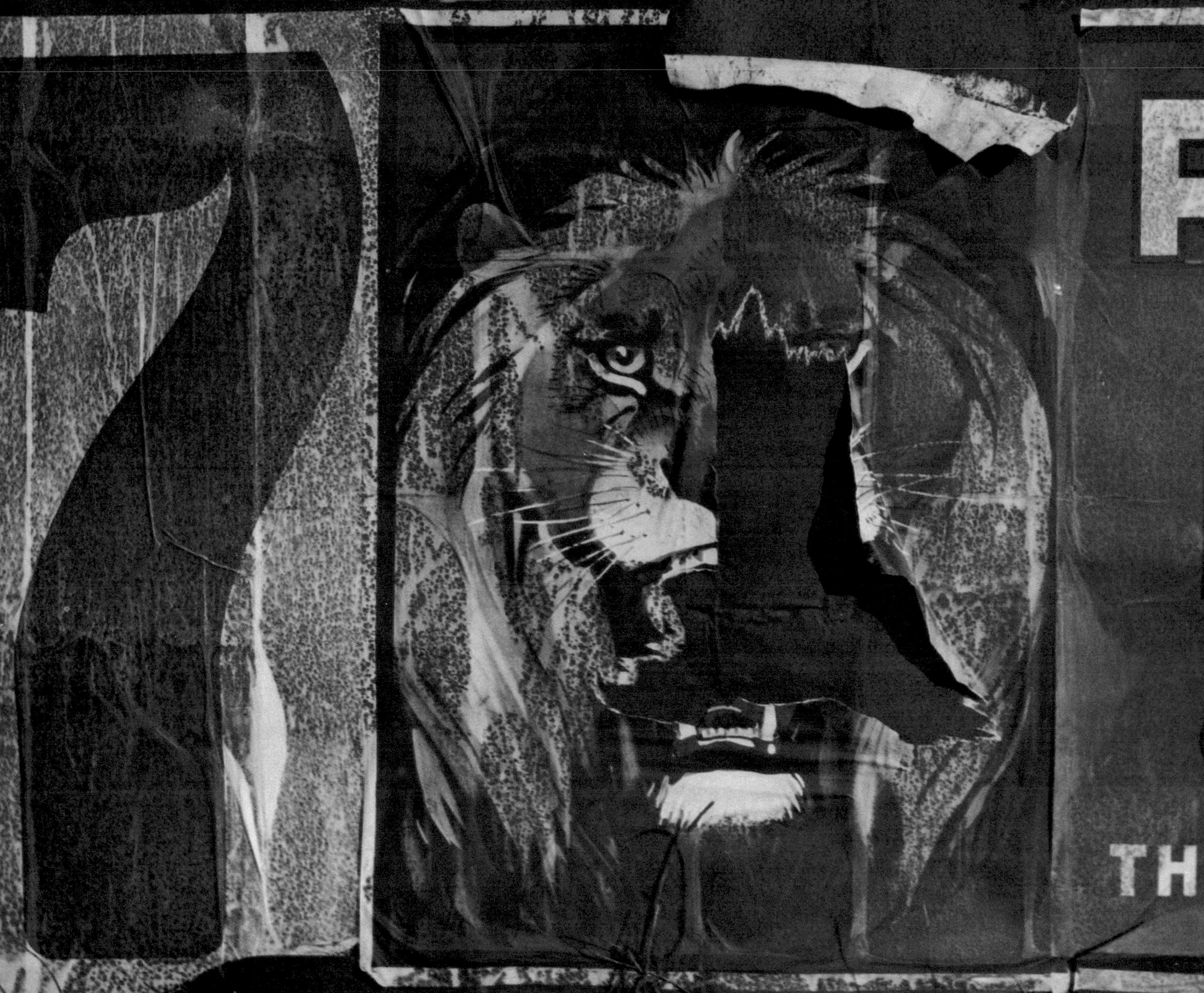
TH

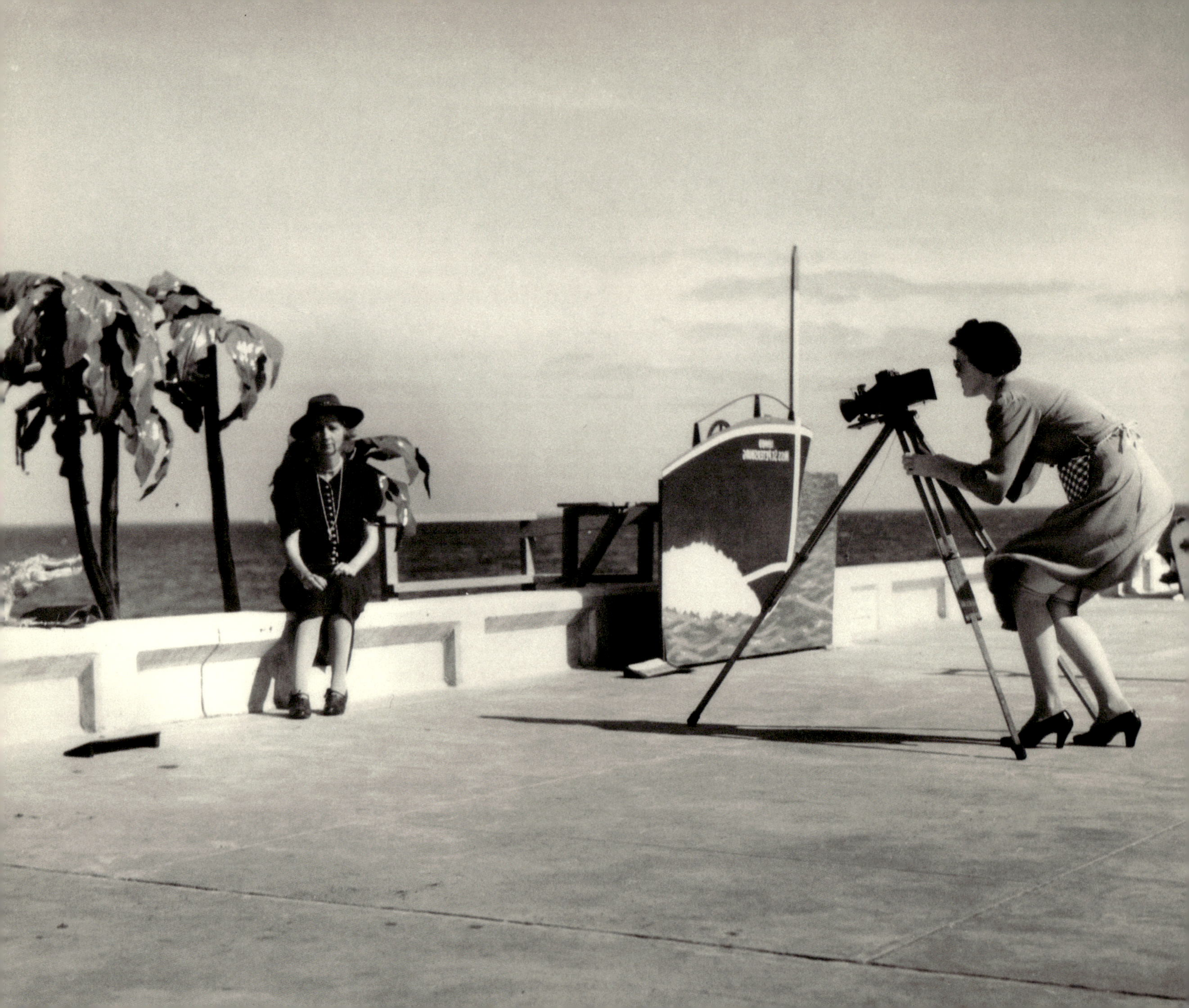

WALKER EVANS

Florida

With an essay by
Robert Plunket

The J. Paul Getty Museum ✻ Los Angeles

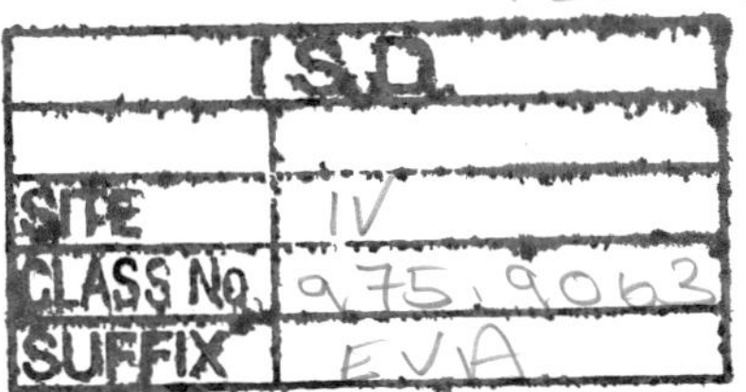

Introduction:

Evans in Florida, 1941

Longtime newspaperman Karl Bickel retired with his wife to Sarasota, Florida, in 1935. Bickel had been president of what was then called United Press Associations (now UPI) from 1923 to 1935, had written the book *New Empires: The Newspaper and the Radio* (1930), and, in 1932, had confidentially advised Charles Lindbergh on how to deal with the media during the ordeal of his son's kidnapping. In the quiet resort town of Sarasota (population 8,000), Bickel quickly became a community leader working toward economic as well as cultural improvements. He also took up the hobby of investigating the history of the west coast of the state. The result of his research was *The Mangrove Coast: The Story of the West Coast of Florida.* It is a book that ranges from the geology of the region to the legends of its explorers to the author's personal reminiscences about favorite fishing trips.

The Mangrove Coast concerns a stretch of the state along the Gulf of Mexico described by Bickel as extending "from Ancolote Anchorage to Sanibel Key and then tapering off from Sanibel southward to the distant mouth of the Shark." Bickel declares that the attraction of the Mangrove Coast is actually to be found, not in its past, but "in its intangibles: the gleam of white sand, the softness of southwest winds, pink and turquoise sunsets, and the abiding simplicity of its people."

It does seem strange that Walker Evans (1903–1975), a photographer who consistently maintained that he found nature uninteresting, was selected to provide illustrations for a book about the historical myths and natural beauty of the nation's vacationland, its southernmost state. But whatever the reasons for the offer, Evans was happy to accept the job of illustrating Bickel's book, which involved a six-week trip to Florida in 1941 and paid him a much-needed fee.

The Mangrove Coast appeared in 1942 in a first edition that consisted of Bickel's text (with an epilogue written that January reflecting the recent effects of wartime on Florida's west coast), followed by a portfolio of thirty-two photographs by Evans, introduced with his captions. This group of pictures is possibly the least known of Evans's pre-1945 works and survives in very few 1940s prints, most of them now located at the Getty Museum. Their importance has been overshadowed by Evans's New York subway series of the same period, but they exhibit the photographer's eye in an equally exceptional way and, with more exposure, should be accepted as a significant phase in the development of Evans's mature documentary style, comparable to his 1933 work in Cuba and his Depression-era pictures "from the field" for the Resettlement Administration.

The selection of Evans's Florida photographs presented here is accompanied by an essay by novelist Robert Plunket, who lives in Sarasota. Mr. Plunket knows Florida intimately, and his wry assessment of the Bickel–Evans collaboration places these little-known photographs within the colorful context of the Mangrove Coast.

Judith Keller
Associate Curator
Department of Photographs

A Technical Note

Walker Evans: Florida *contains fifty-four gelatin silver photographs, a number of which were first published in Karl Bickel's* The Mangrove Coast *(1942). All of the images were selected from the Getty Museum's collection, the largest holding of prints made by Walker Evans himself. A few of the photographs have been slightly cropped, and a very few have been significantly cropped. All of the photographs are reproduced in their complete form, with their dimensions and accession numbers, beginning on page 64. Further information about the prints, as well as the entire Getty collection of Evans's work, can be found in my* Walker Evans: The Getty Museum Collection *(1995).*

J.K.

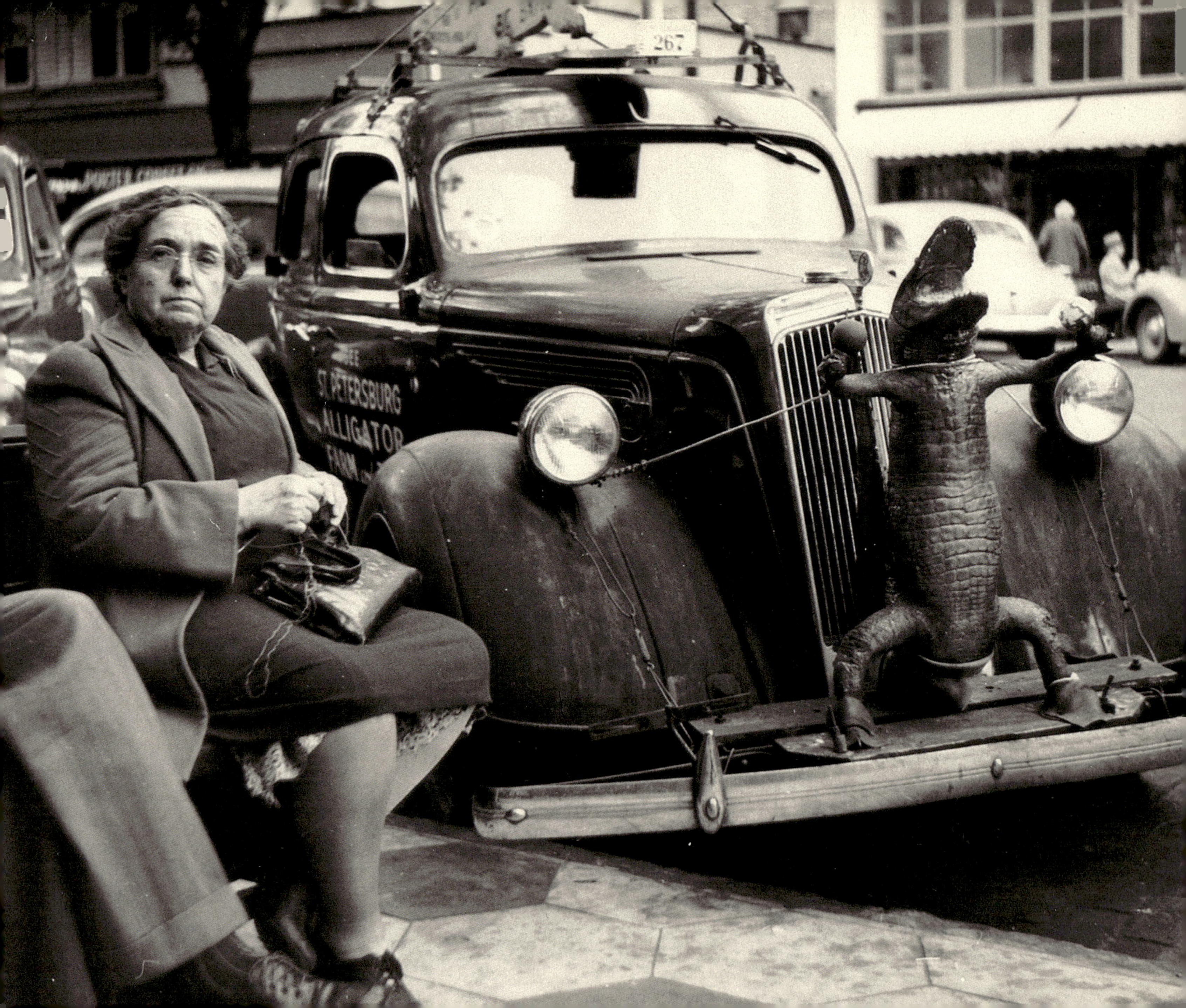
267
ST. PETERSBURG
ALLIGATOR
FARM

It is not to be denied
that full half of the
tourists and travellers
that come to Florida
return intensely
disappointed, and
even disgusted.

Why?

—Harriet Beecher Stowe
Palmetto Leaves, 1873

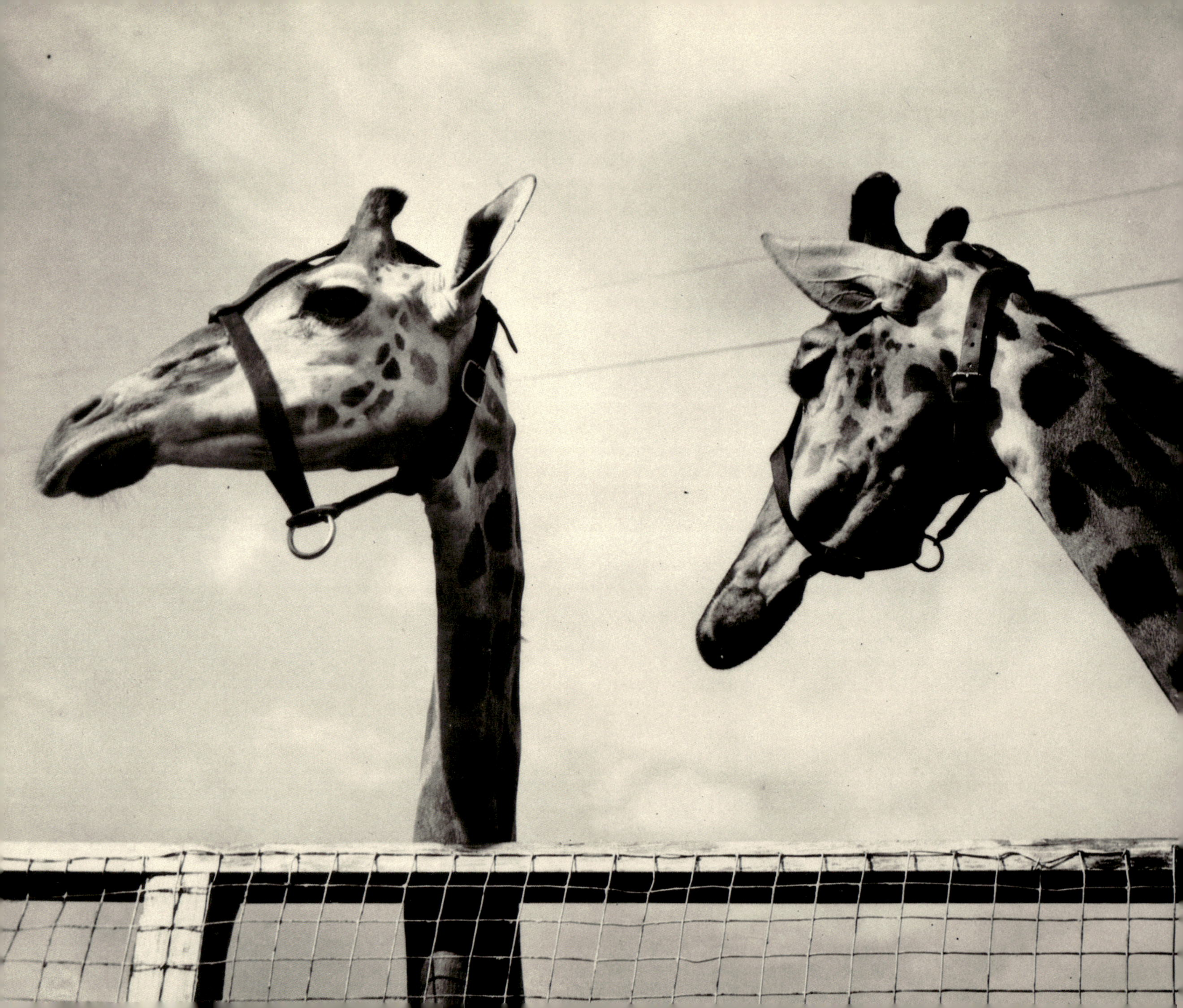

Walker Evans, the Mangrove Coast, and Me

by Robert Plunket

Call me Mr. Chatterbox.

Just about everyone in Sarasota does. For the past fifteen years I have been one of the town's leading gossip columnists. I've covered everything from charity balls to the Mayor's Prayer Breakfast, from the high-school prom to the opening night of the French Film Festival, where Jeanne Moreau and Audrey Hepburn, dressed to the nines, vied for "best entrance." (Audrey won.) I've roasted politicians, I've emceed charity auctions, I've modeled sportswear to benefit the Humane Society. I've even interviewed Warren Burger and Pia Zadora, although not at the same time.

PAGE xii
Two Giraffes, Circus Winter Quarters, Sarasota

PAGE 3
Concrete Block Building with Shell Decoration

And in doing so I've learned a lot about Florida. It really is different down here—the way it looks, the weather, the social patterns, the brand-newness of the place. Everybody comes from somewhere else, which means he has secrets from his past back in Dayton, and in a number of cases those secrets involve former wives who disappeared under mysterious circumstances. An amazing number of people blow into town, make a splashy name for themselves, and then are arrested. The buying and selling of real estate is the dominant industry. Indeed, it could be said that the real-estate ad is the principal form of literature here.

Even the art is different. True, there is much conventional art—paintings, performances, etc. But the really interesting artistic endeavors are usually disguised as something else—a theme park, a mystery novel, a coconut, even a simple vacation photograph. Walker Evans took many photographs here in 1941, but they are not, definitely not, vacation photographs. They are something else entirely.

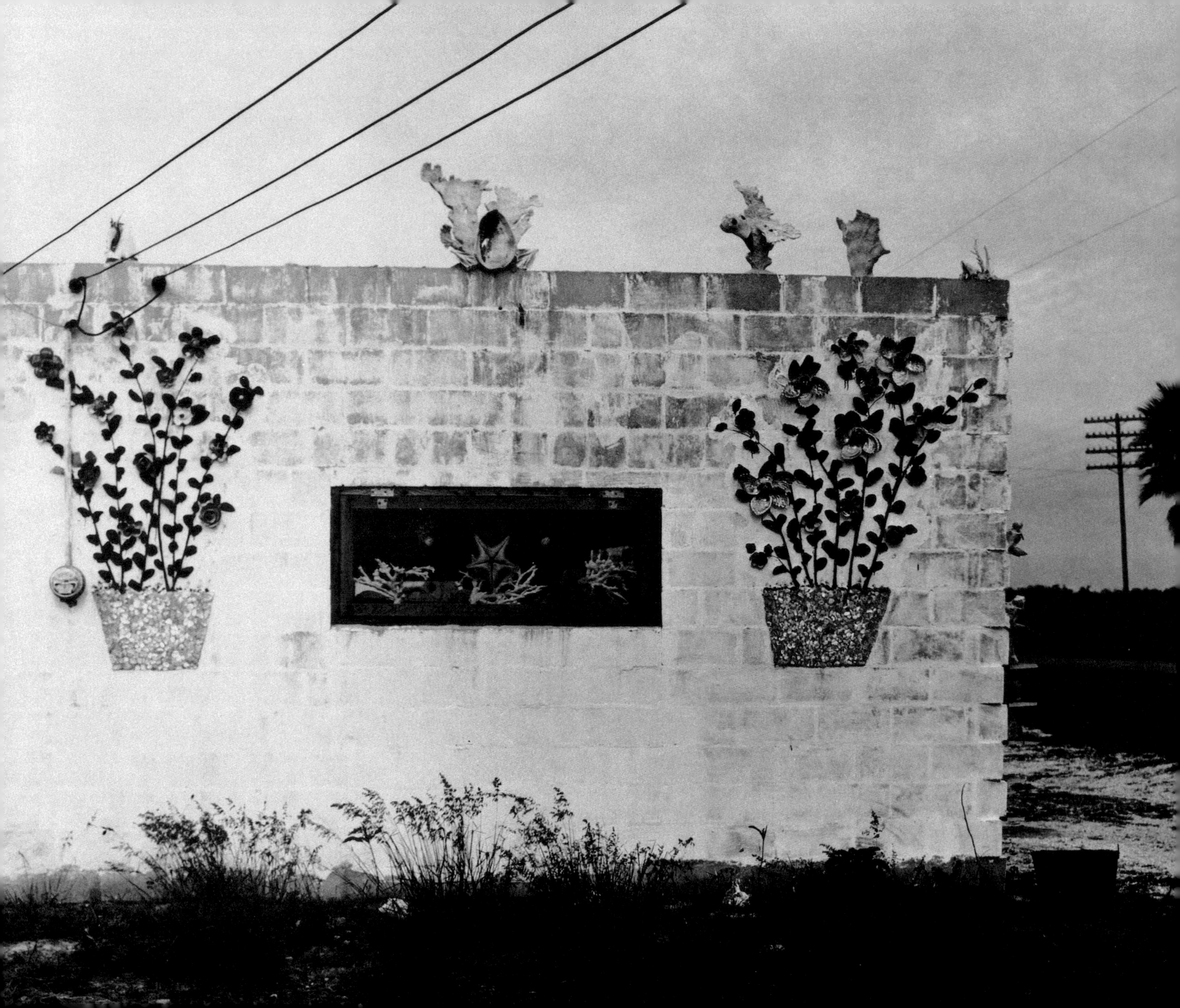

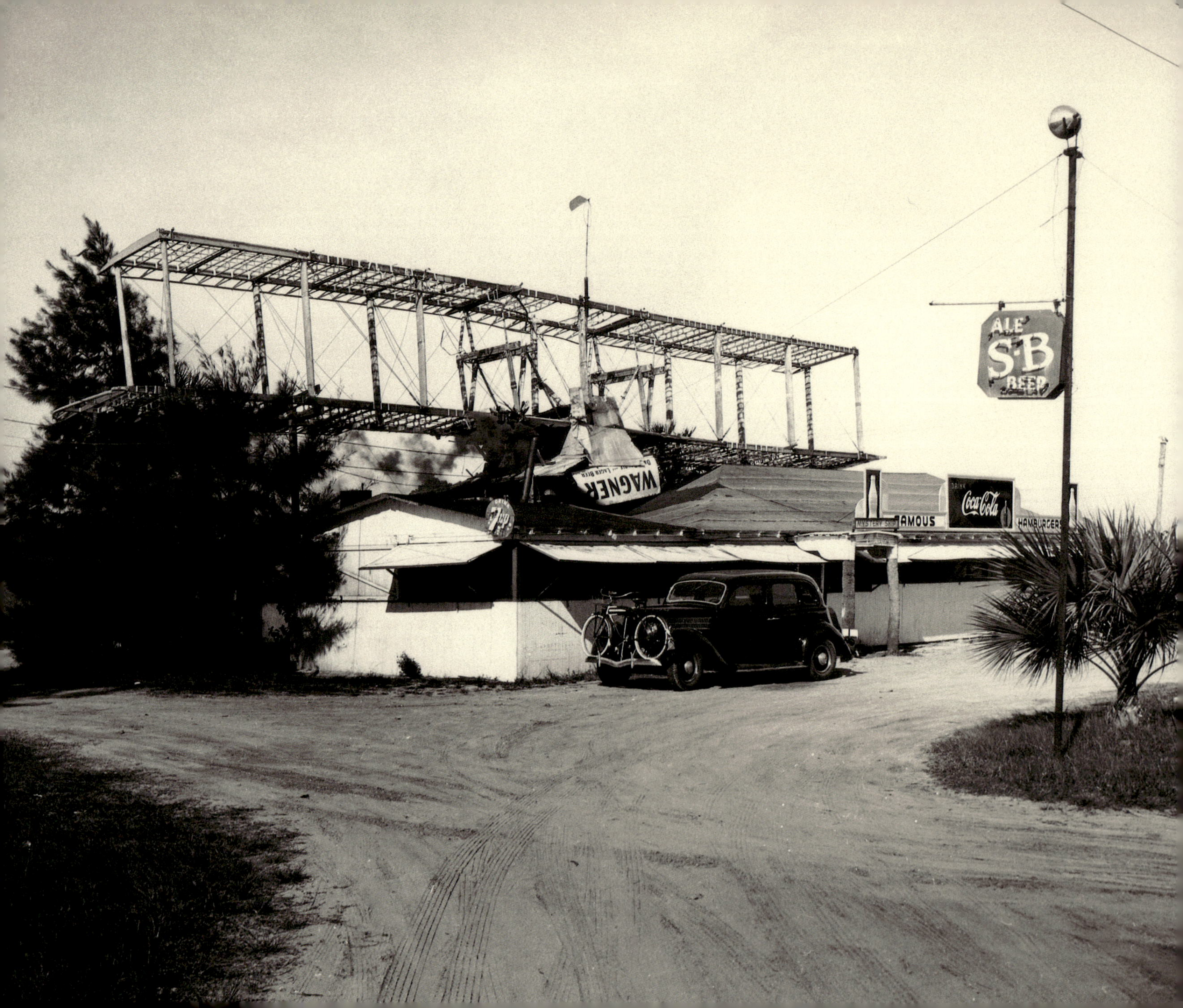
ALE
S·B
BEER
WAGNER
DRINK
Coca-Cola
AMOUS
HAMBURGERS

OPPOSITE
Mystery Ship Roadside Bar

I first became interested in Walker Evans because I am what you might call a biography freak. They are my favorite form of reading. I haunt the "New Books" section at Selby Library at least once a week, looking for the latest. I'll read anything, but I find myself most drawn to the lives of those tortured twentieth-century American writers, the ones who smoke and drank too much and then died young, thus becoming instant legends. One thing I've noticed is that in an astonishing number of these books, the name Walker Evans keeps popping up.

Two of Evans's closest friends have particularly interested me. The first was

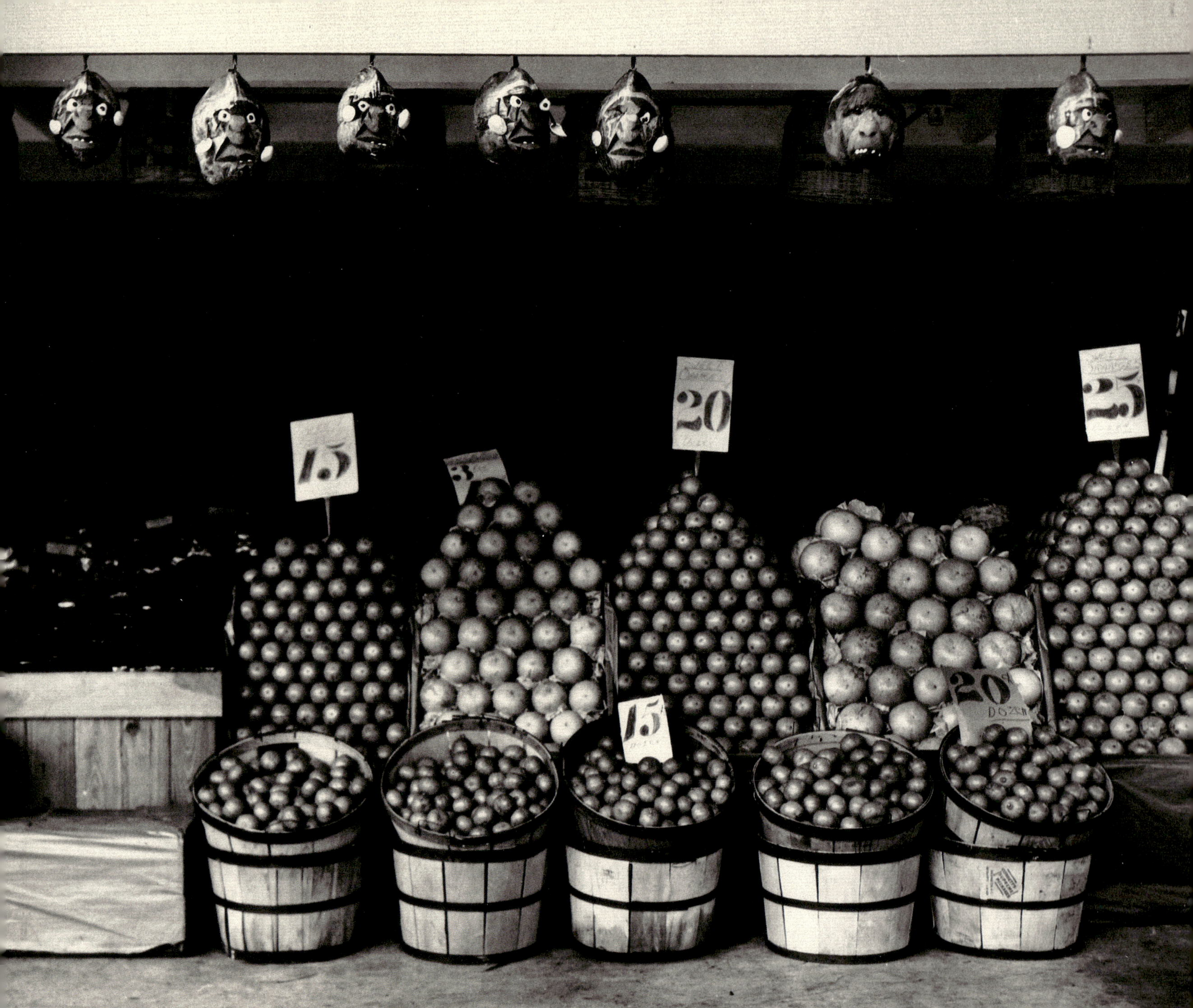

15
20
25
15
20
DOZEN

OPPOSITE
Souvenir Shop Display

RIGHT
Racetrack Spectators

Hart Crane, one of the great poets of the twenties. Talk about intense: he worked on one poem for seven years—*The Bridge*—for which Evans took the frontispiece photograph. Crane was a binge drinker and an indefatigable sailor-chaser, that is, until he surprised everyone by running off with Malcolm Cowley's wife. They went to Mexico and moved in with Katherine Anne Porter. But on the way back, Crane had second thoughts and jumped ship, literally, leaping off the stern of the SS *Orizaba* and drowning just north of Havana.

James Agee was even stranger. His career was the triumph of the will.

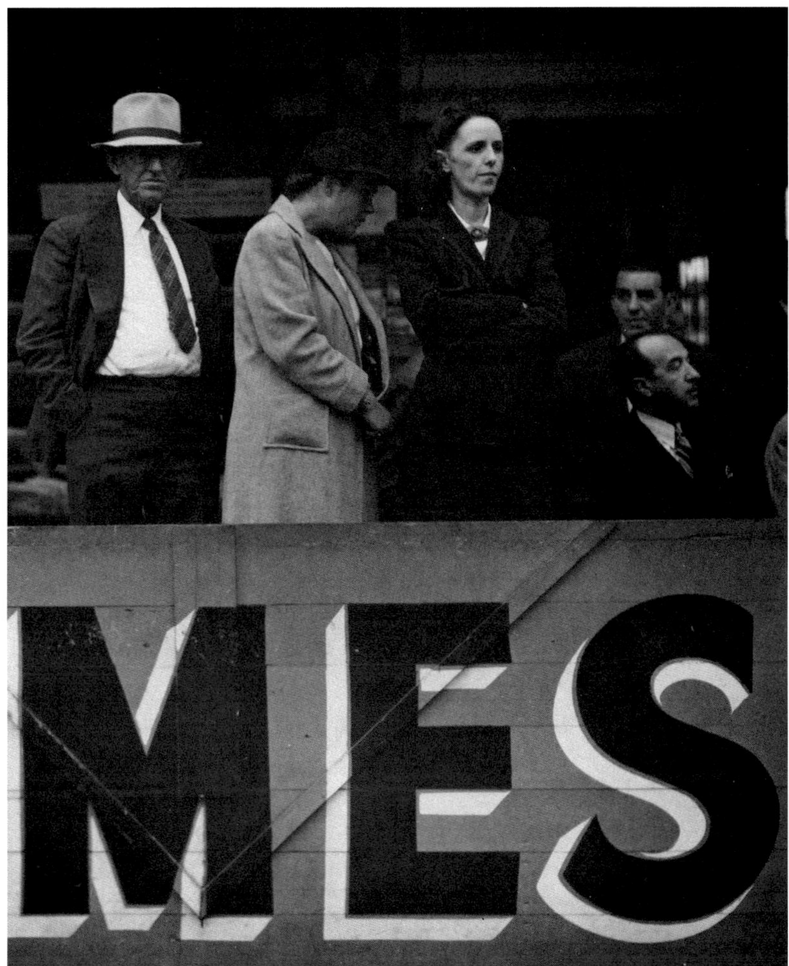

Nobody wanted to be a great writer more that he. He published one very good novel, *A Death in the Family*, more or less to prove that he could, but he is best remembered for his collaboration with Evans, *Let Us Now Praise Famous Men*, and his screenplay for *The African Queen*. Like Crane he died young, a heart attack in a taxicab. He was literally worn out by art. He was one of the original "problem smokers"; he had a bad heart but couldn't stop his constant intake of nicotine. Women found him very sexy in a Nicolas Cage sort of way, and as he is a biographer's dream, there are quite a few books about him.

Evans is the mystery of the trio. One reason may be that he lacked the energy of his friends. He was cool, passive, shy, more a voyeur than a participant. Evans didn't wear his heart on his sleeve like Crane and Agee. He loved people-watching, particularly when he could do it in a reclining position. Today there are many artists like him—Andy Warhol and R. Crumb leap to mind—but Walker Evans was, back in the '30s and '40s, ahead of his time, personality-wise.

An example: he embraced the commercial. Indeed, his career was one of moving from job to job. Most of his major work resulted from becoming attached to a project initiated by some-

Now, in his new home, Karl set out to become Sarasota's ideal citizen, the "active retiree."

one else. The best known was, of course, *Let Us Now Praise Famous Men*. But there were others as well; the book you're holding in your hands is the result of one of Evans's more exotic assignments, and just about the only one that could be described as fun.

It all began when Evans was contacted on behalf of a man named Karl Bickel, who needed some photographs for a book he was writing. Bickel had recently retired to Sarasota after a long and distinguished career in journalism that started with his coverage of the San Francisco earthquake. He moved from strength to strength until he ended up as head of UPI.

He joined various civic boards and boosted the city. He led the drive to build a big pavilion out at Lido Beach, and his wife, Madira, is still remembered for her ironfisted rule of the local women's club. But they both had an intellectual side as well, and the history of Florida became their specialty. Indeed, Madira rose to such prominence in the state historical society that an ancient Indian midden, or pile of shells, is named in her honor up in Terra Ceia.

Karl decided to do her one better, though. He would write a book detailing the long and colorful history of the Gulf Coast of Florida, to be titled *The Mangrove Coast,* after the ubiquitous plant that grows half-in and half-out of the water and covers much of

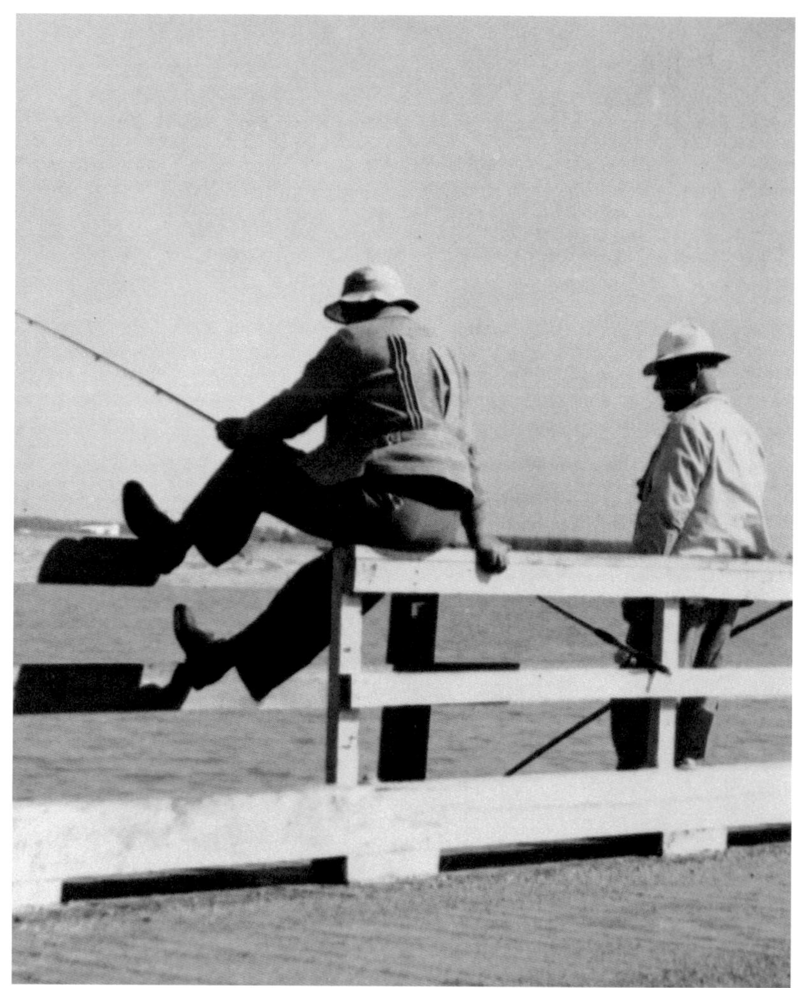

LEFT
Two Men Fishing

OPPOSITE
Shuffleboard Players

the shoreline. And he would get a first-rate photographer to supply the pictures. Walker Evans, who was, after all, the first photographer to be honored with an exhibit at the Museum of Modern Art, sounded perfect.

With his Guggenheim money running out (he'd received a fellowship in 1940) and the release of *Let Us Now Praise Famous Men* so disappointing—the book sold a mere six hundred copies—Evans must have been very happy with the prospect of spending six weeks in Florida, all expenses paid, just as cold was settling in up North. Furthermore it would be a free honeymoon: Evans had just married Jane Smith Ninas, a painter. And so, in late October of 1941, the newlyweds set out for the west coast of Florida.

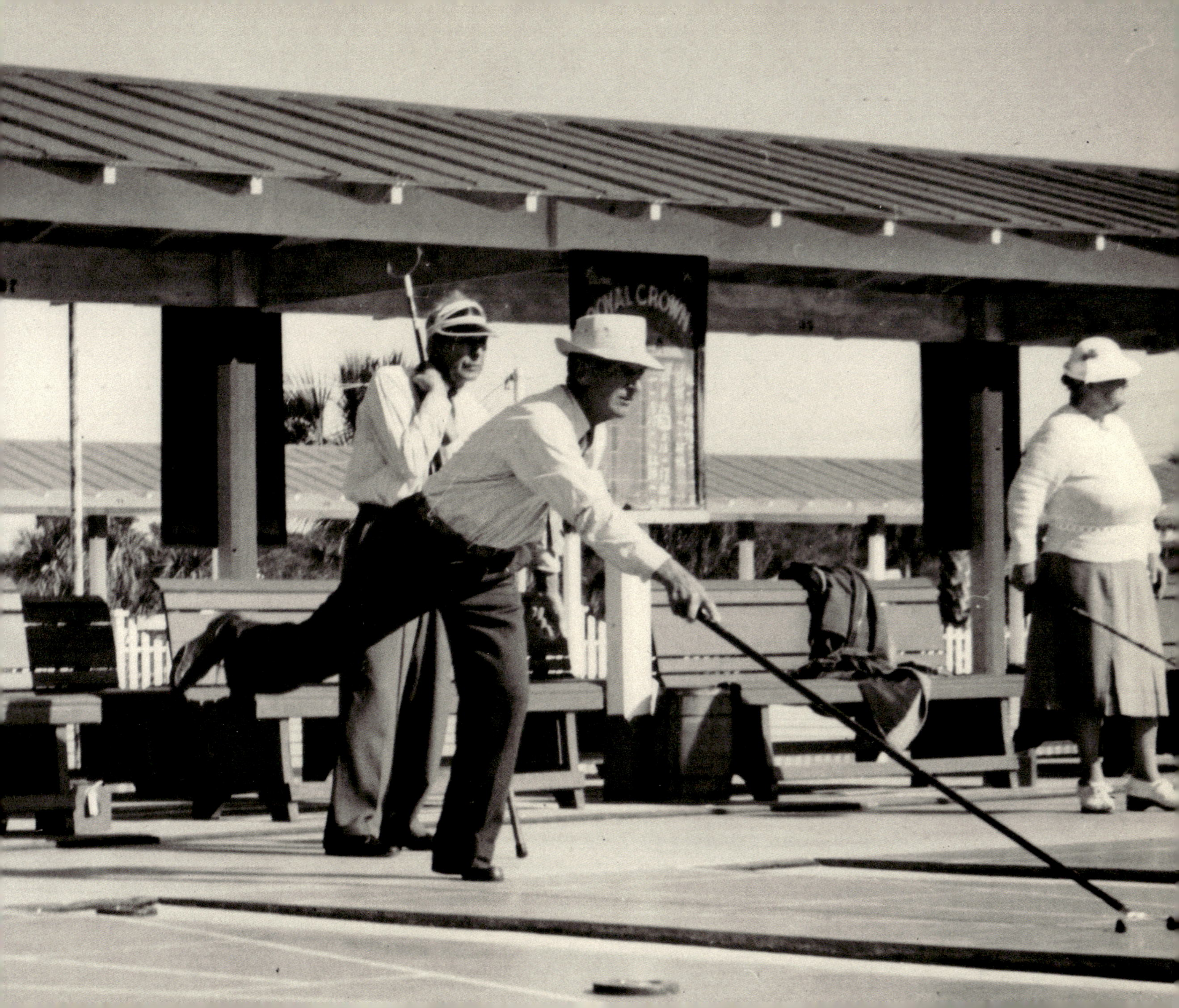
CROWN

If the phrase "west coast of Florida" is drawing a blank in your mind, don't worry: even people on the east coast of Florida don't know much about it. You grow up on one coast and spend your entire life there, without going to the other. One reason is the journey itself, an endless drive through swamp or sugarcane or cattle ranches. The only human settlements are migrant-worker and prison camps. The message is clear: behave, or you'll end up in the middle of the state.

No one denies that the east coast is more glamorous. It always has been. There was nothing quite as exciting as Miami Beach in the 1950s, and now, in its new guise, the Beach is back on top, with all those hip models and no place to park. And Palm Beach has always been one of the most glamorous places in the world, a top-ten contender. Even Boca Raton, even Ft. Lauderdale. . . .

But Tampa?

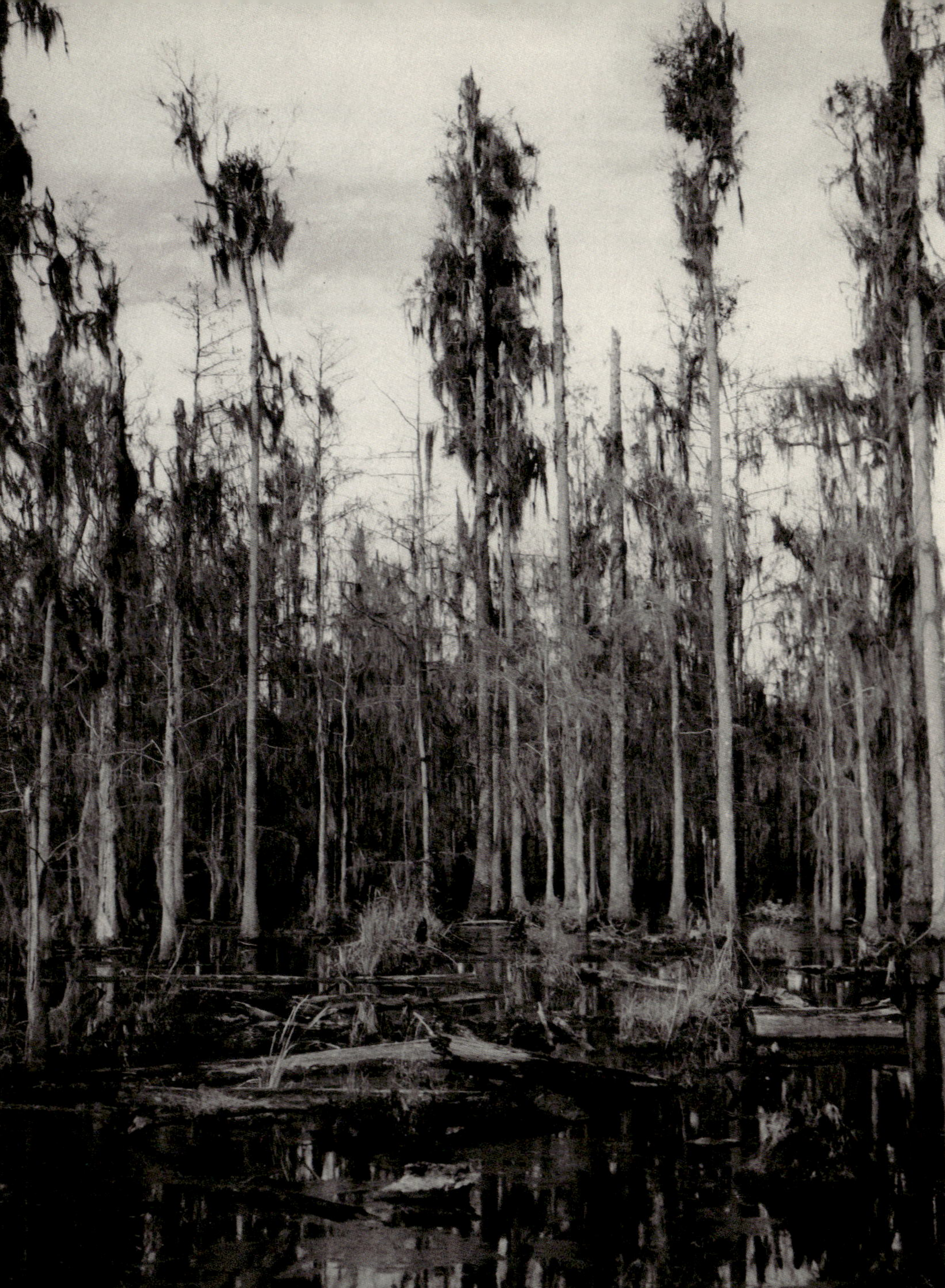

LEFT
Cypress Swamp

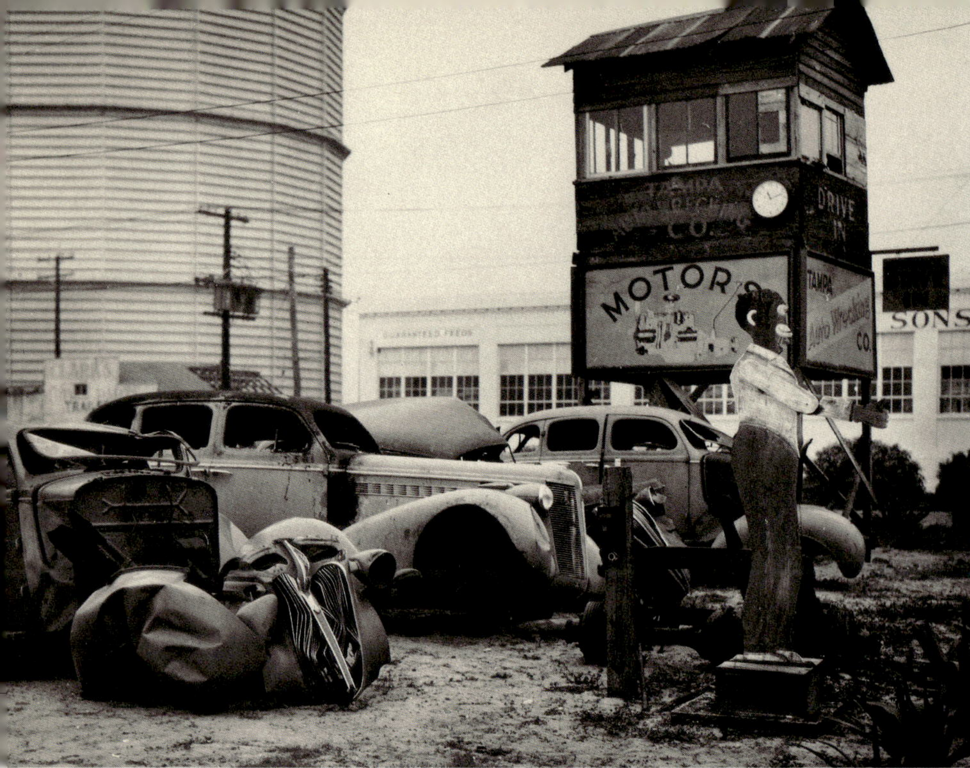

Like any self-respecting place with a similar problem, the west coast concedes glamour but insists that it is more "real." In this case, "real" means real old and real quiet, and with an indigenous population that is real Southern in thought and action and lifestyle (i.e., lots of pickup trucks with Confederate flags). The economy centers around the retirement industry, and anyone under fifty is perceived as startlingly young. Though there are pockets of affluence (Naples and, near Sarasota, Longboat Key), the general atmosphere is middle-class Midwestern, with palm trees.

Keep in mind that the west coast of Florida is not the same thing as the Gulf Coast. The Gulf Coast stretches from Pensacola, at the Alabama border, all the way south to the end of the mainland, just north of Key West. The west coast is the lower part of the Gulf Coast, the part that faces west; up in the Panhandle, the land faces south. These two parts of the Gulf Coast, like the east and west coasts, have nothing to do with each other and are, in fact, separated by another natural barrier. On the map it looks like an enormous mangrove swamp. Whatever it is, it is impenetrable, and no one ever goes there.

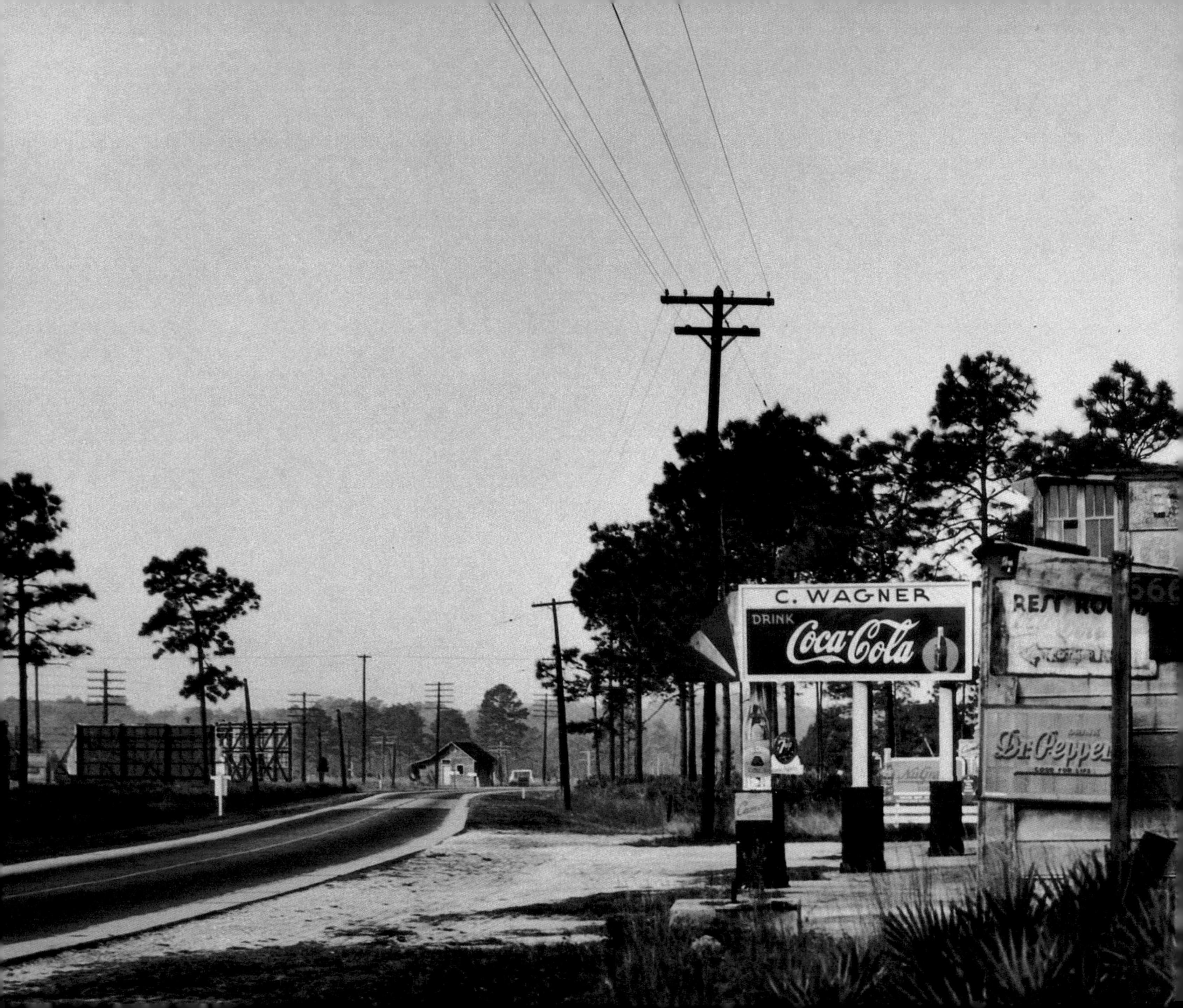
C. WAGNER
DRINK
Coca-Cola

PAGE 14
Auto Graveyard at Tampa

PAGE 15
Upstate Roadside Landscape

RIGHT
Fishermen in Sponge Boat, Tarpon Springs

OPPOSITE
Sponge-Diver's Boat, Tarpon Springs

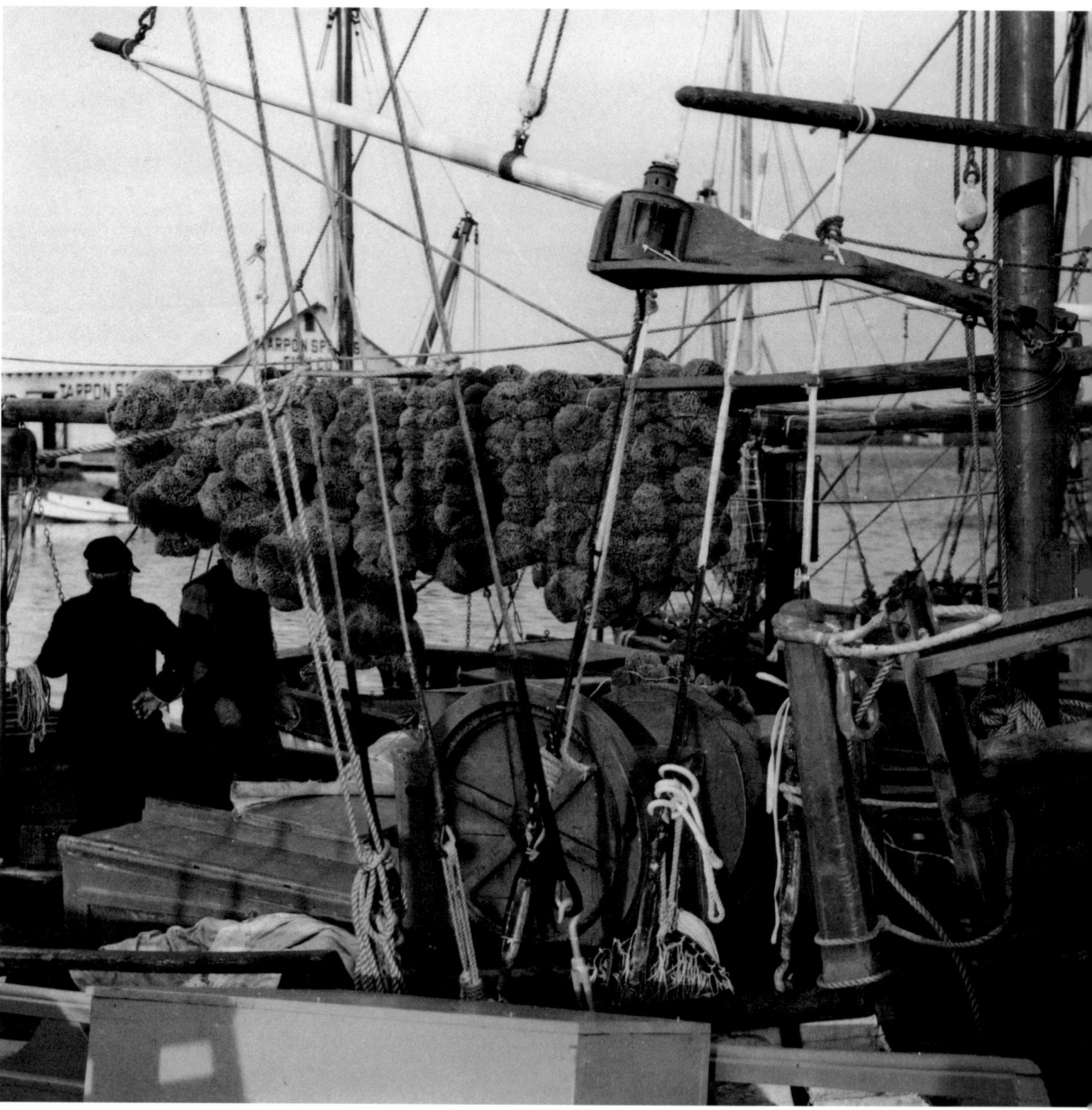

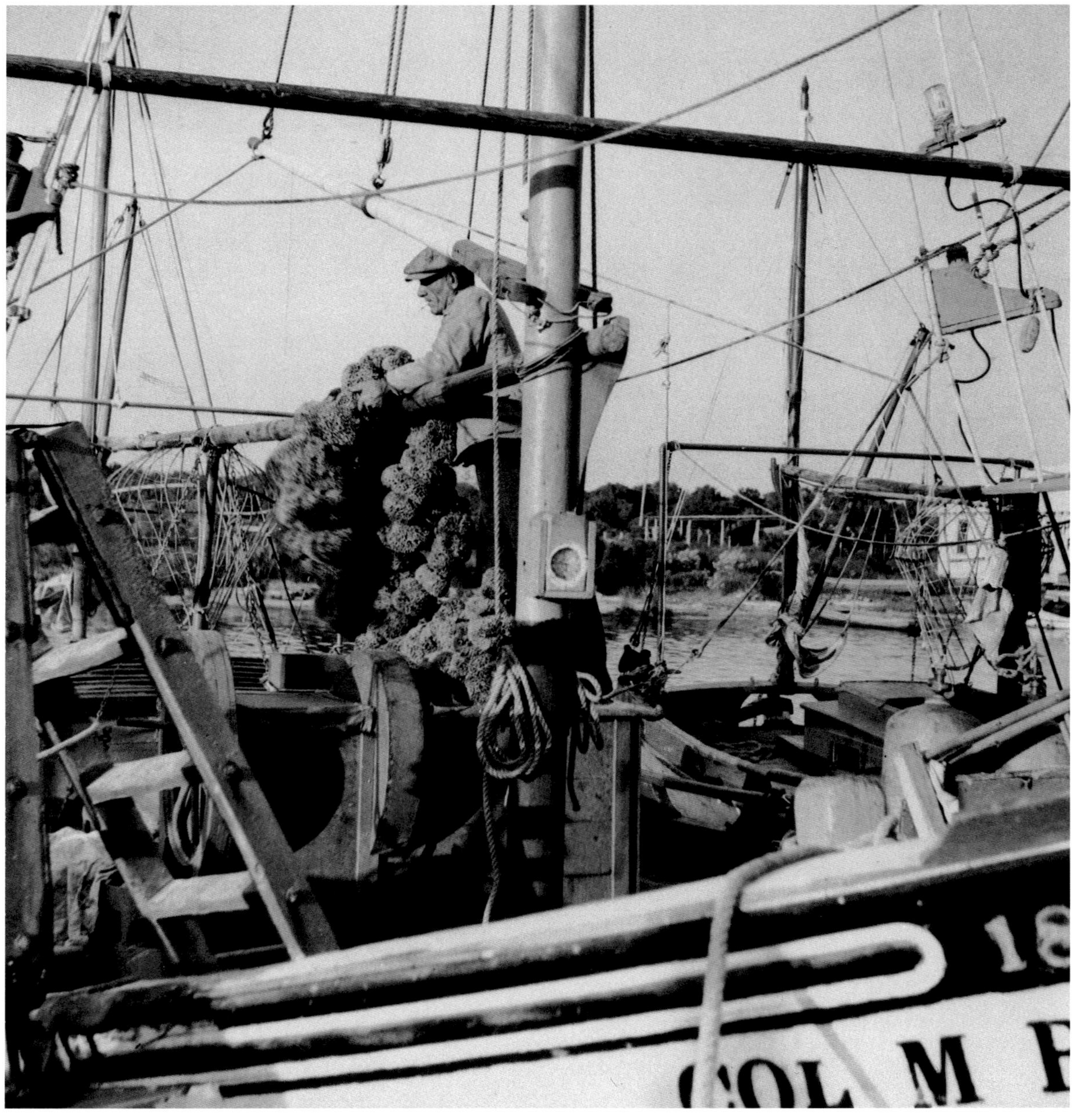
18
COL M

The west coast, where Evans took all his photographs, begins north of Tampa with a smattering of little towns, the most interesting of which is Tarpon Springs, where fifth-generation Greeks dive for sponges. Next comes Tampa itself. On the surface it seems to be a large commercial center of no particular interest, but the more you study it, the more it becomes very interesting indeed. Criminals on the lam are always being caught in motels there, and a serious devil-worship problem exists among the young; yet another claim to fame is that it has the highest incidence of lightning strikes in the country. St. Petersburg, across the bay, functions as a glum Brooklyn to Tampa's Manhattan. It was here that a broken, barely middle-aged Jack Kerouac drank himself to death in his mother's house.

Heading south, we next encounter Bradenton, an old Southern town famous as the home of Tropicana Orange Juice.

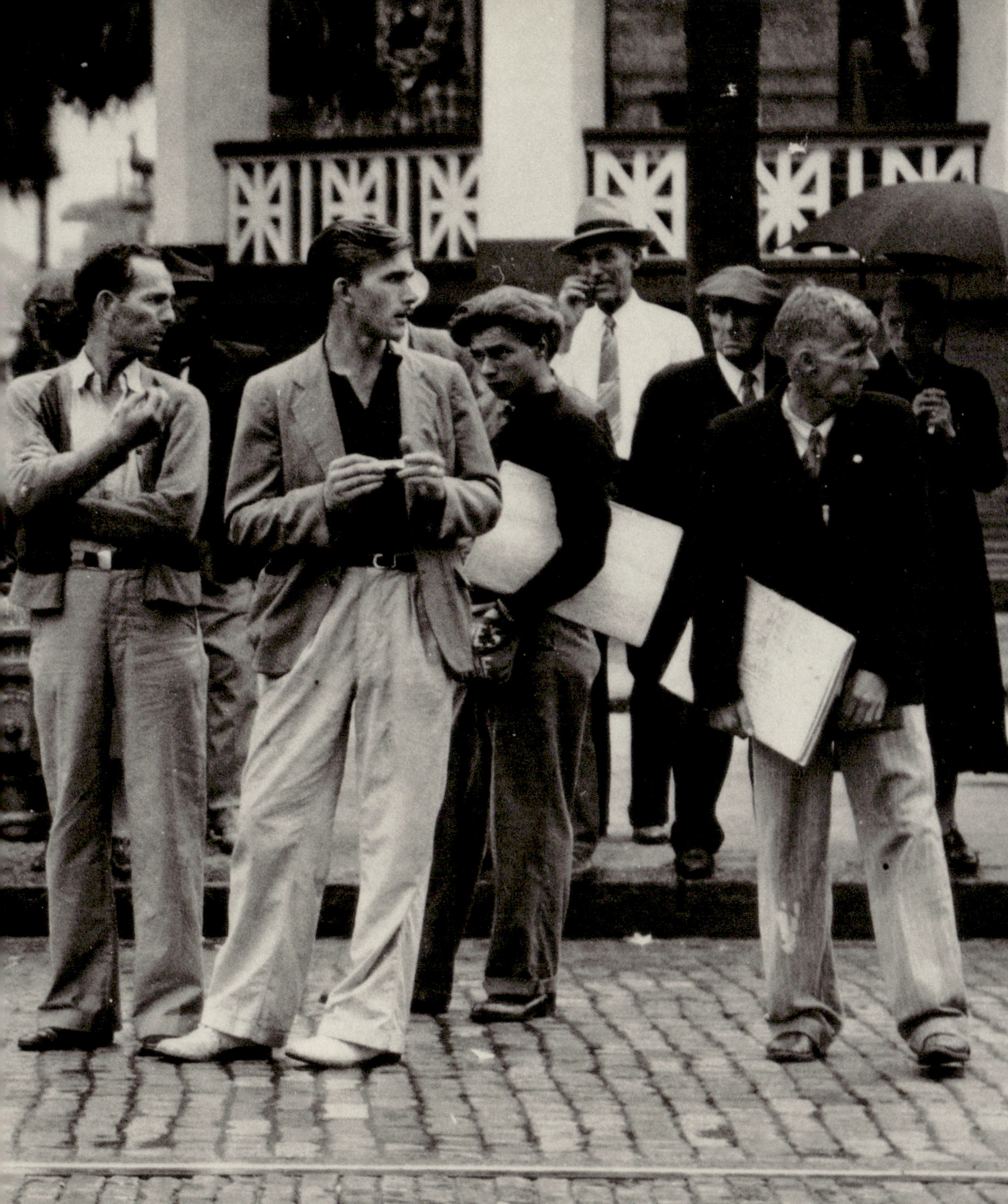

LEFT
Crowd Waiting at Street Corner, Tampa

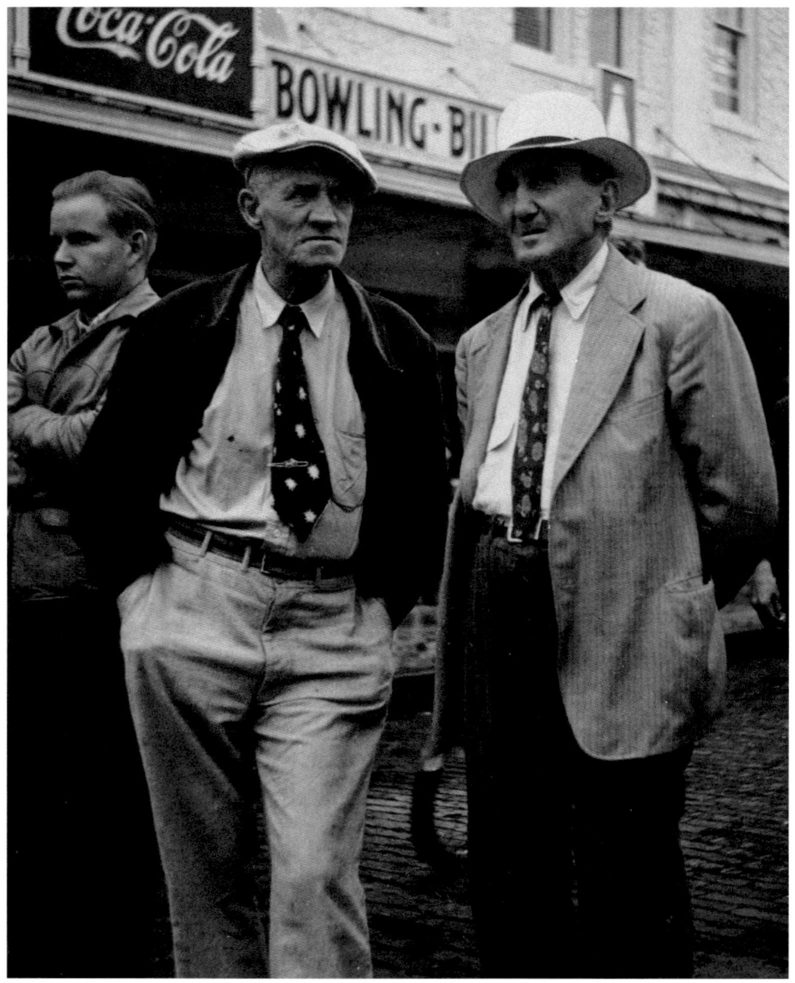

Then comes Sarasota, about which more later, and then Venice, where retirement has become not just a lifestyle but *the* lifestyle. (I once covered a party there attended by, among others, twenty-seven people over the age of one hundred.) Ft. Myers is next; it is very large, over two hundred thousand inhabitants, but oddly out of the mainstream. I've only had occasion to go there once, and all I can remember is banyan trees and lots of traffic. Next comes Naples, which is very opulent. Old money retires here, but it is smallish—population twenty-one thousand—and, as they say, "dead in the summer." South of Naples is a place called Marco Island, crowded with vacation condos whose charm eludes me, and then . . . nothing.

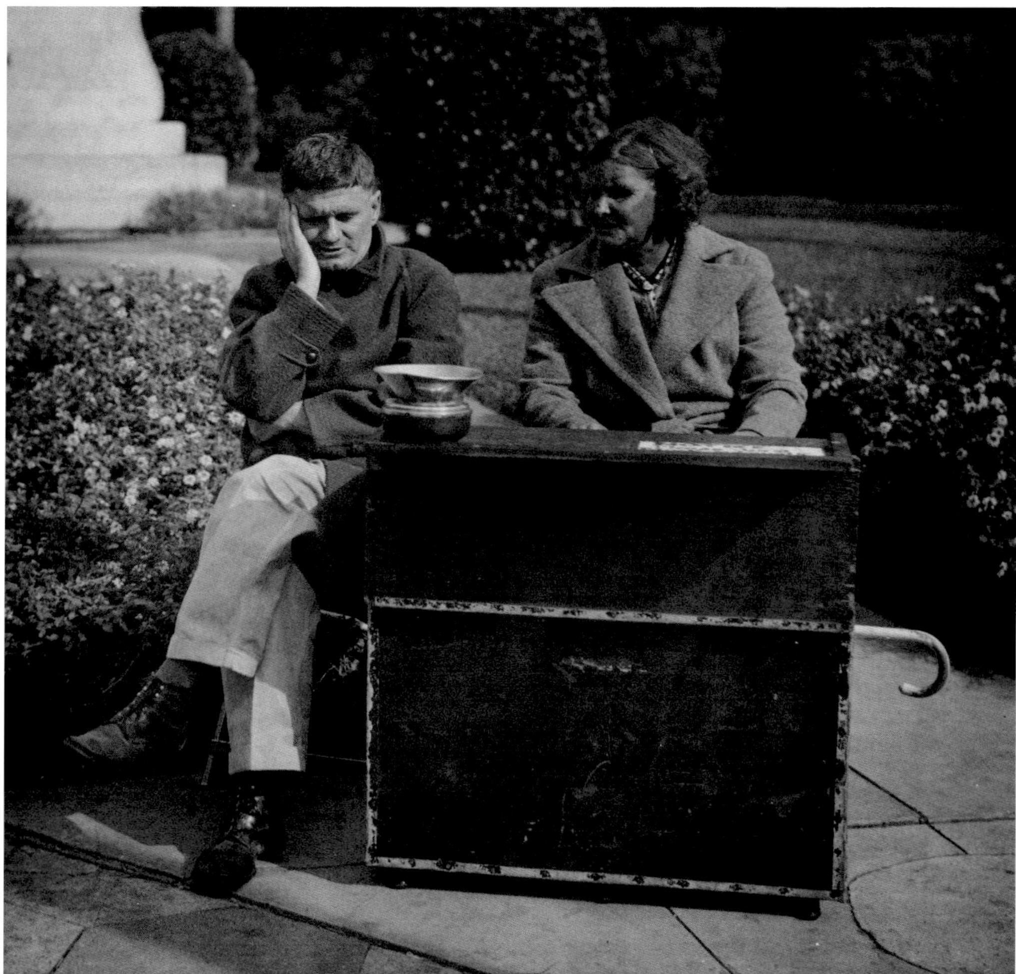

OPPOSITE
Men in the Street at Tampa

LEFT
Blind Couple in Tampa City Square Hall

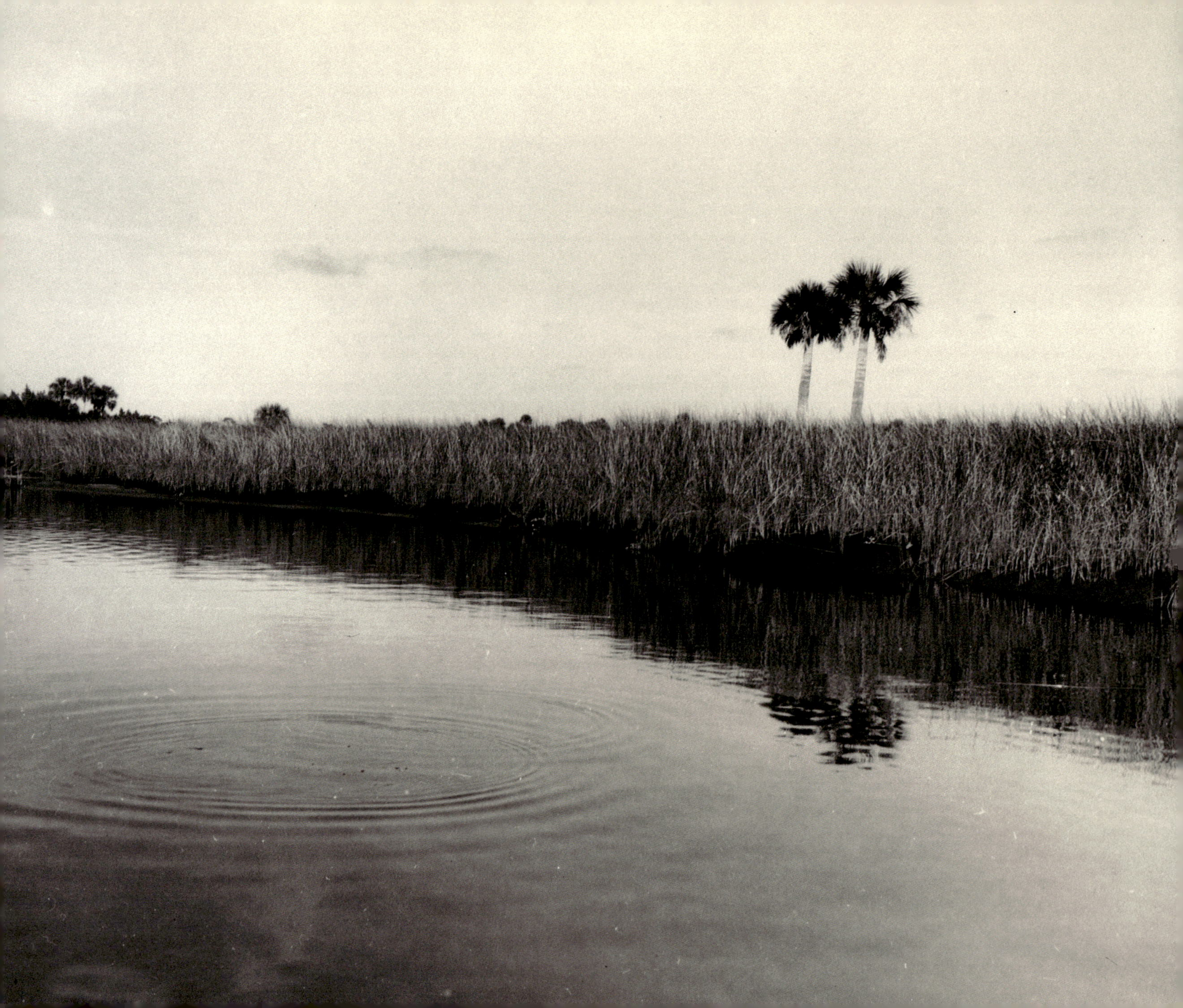

OPPOSITE
Coastal Landscape with Palms

If the west coast of Florida seems a little off the beaten track now, just imagine how isolated it must have seemed back in 1941.

That was before air-conditioning and mosquito control. Roads were few and primitive; much of the transportation was by boat. When Charles and Anne Lindbergh came for a visit, they packed as if for a safari.

But Sarasota was a happy exception to all this. It was world famous back in those days, as the home of the Ringling Bros. and Barnum & Bailey Circus, a beautiful, pristine little town of eight thousand—the undisputed star of the west coast. It had thirty-five miles of white-sand beaches and a cosmopolitan population. The bars must have been great; people still talk about the old Plaza, not to mention the M'Toto Room (named after a famous gorilla) at the El Vernona Hotel, where there were circus acts and dancing every night. Visiting celebrities came through regularly. The Queen of Iran showed up, plus Will Rogers, and even Albert Einstein, who was fitted with a truss at Badger's Drug

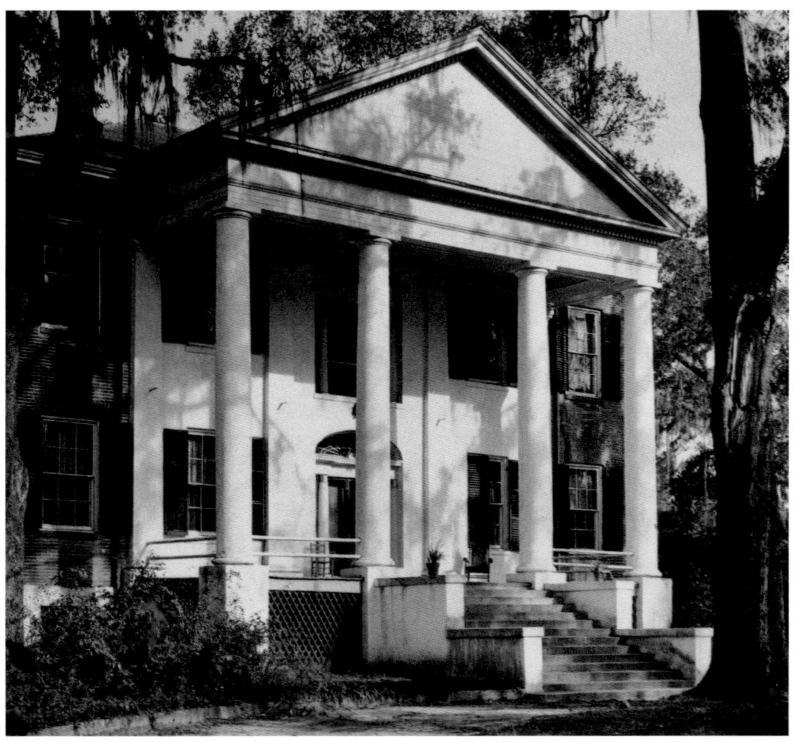

Store on Main Street. The house where he stayed is still standing on South Polk Drive out on Lido Key, making Sarasota one of the few places where we can truly say we had "Einstein on the Beach."

Karl Bickel gave Evans carte blanche as to what to take pictures of, and it's not surprising that the urbane photographer, who bought his clothes at Brooks Brothers, decided to concentrate his efforts on Sarasota. The road trips were few and not very productive. (I wonder if Madira and her middens had anything to do with this.) A journey to Tallahassee* yielded a single portrait of an antebellum mansion and a sidewalk scene. Tampa and St. Pete registered as group portraits of grim, elderly women. Only Tarpon Springs acquitted itself well: Evans loved the diving suit (p. 29) and the amateurish murals (pp. 30–31), versions of which still decorate the Tarpon Springs of today.

*Ralph Waldo Emerson, no less, described Tallahassee as "a grotesque place," settled by "office holders, speculators, and desperados." Even in 1826, few writers were willing to give the west coast a break.

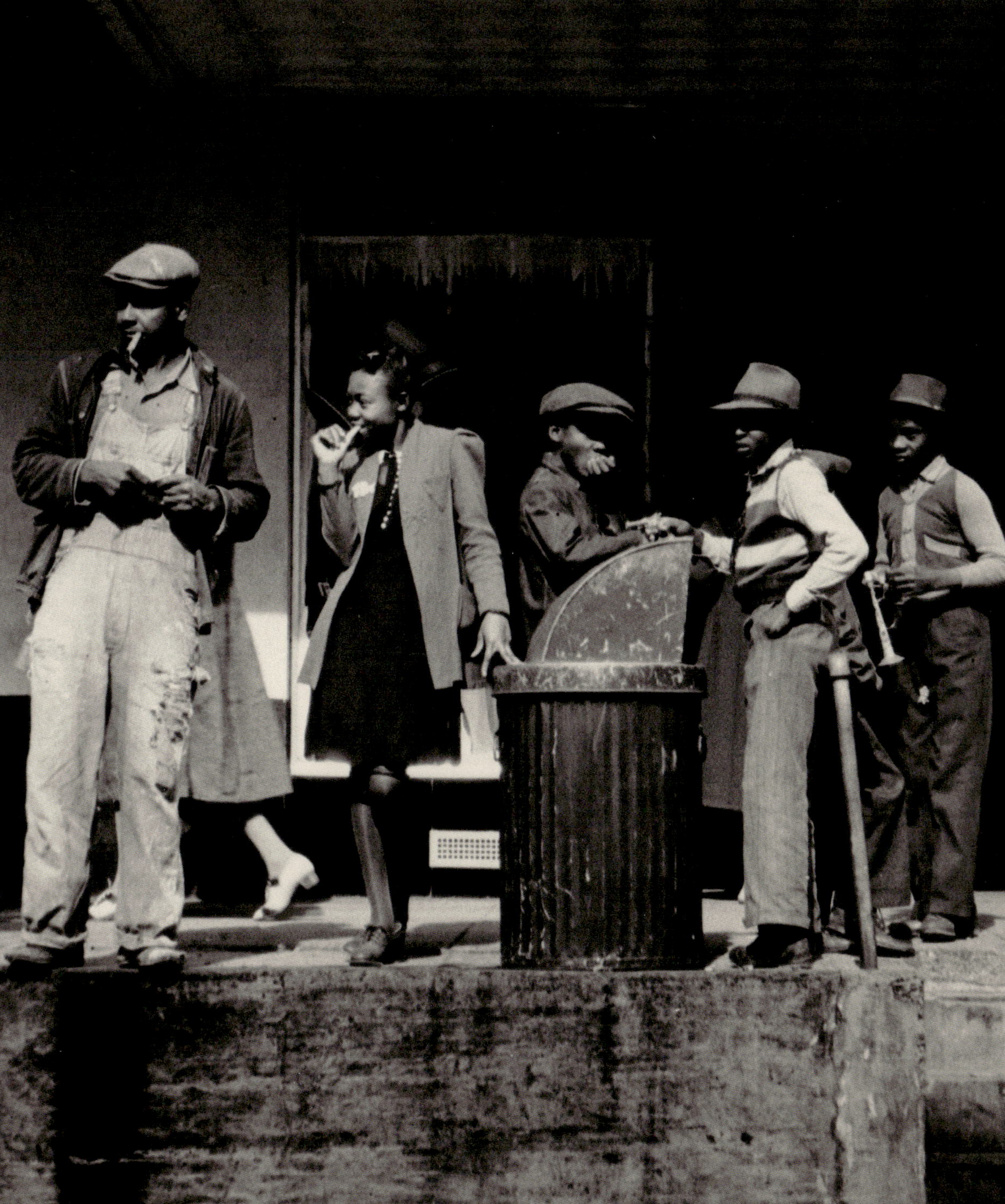

OPPOSITE
Antebellum Plantation House at Tallahassee

LEFT
Negroes at Tallahassee

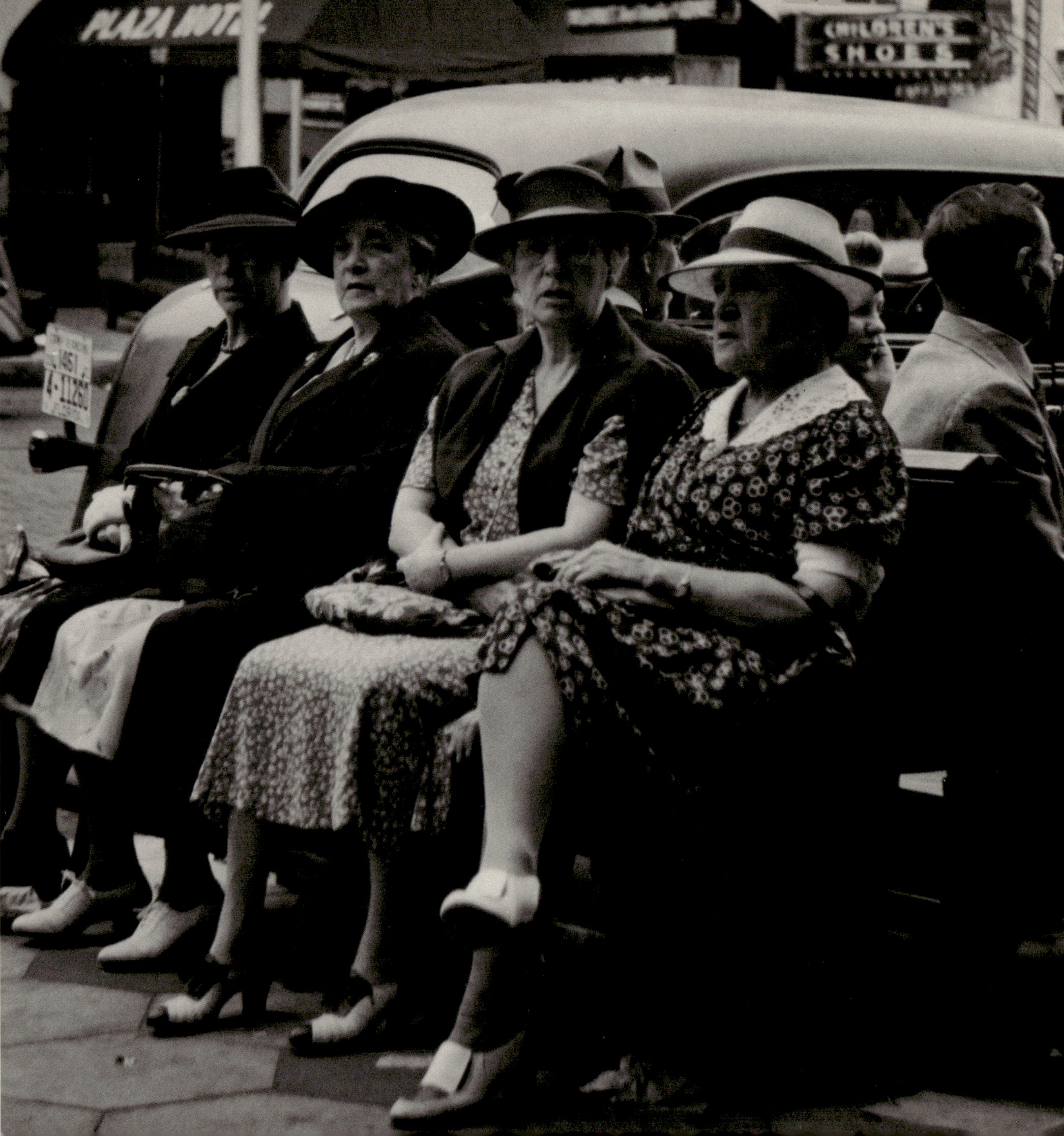
CHILDREN'S
SHOES

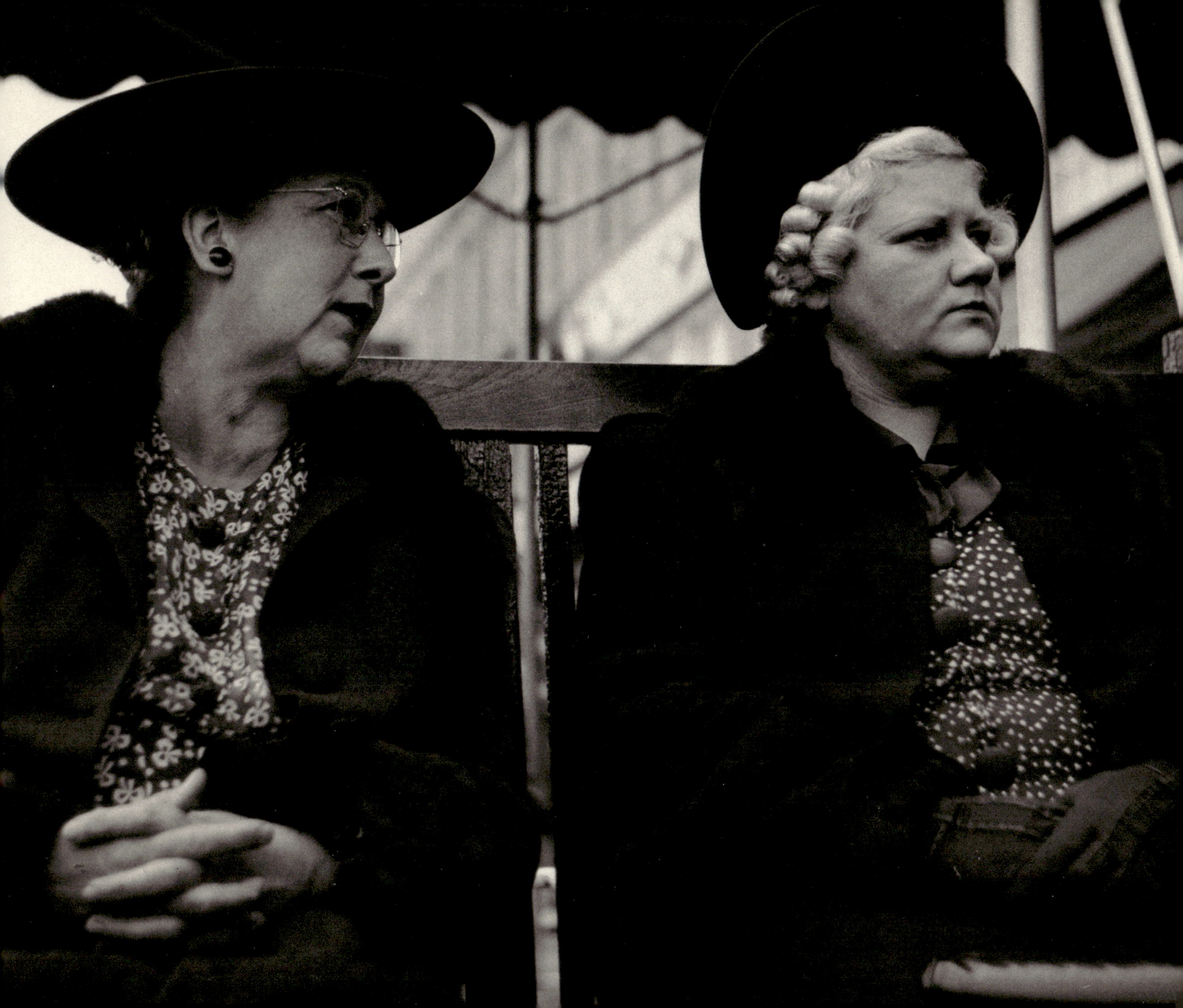

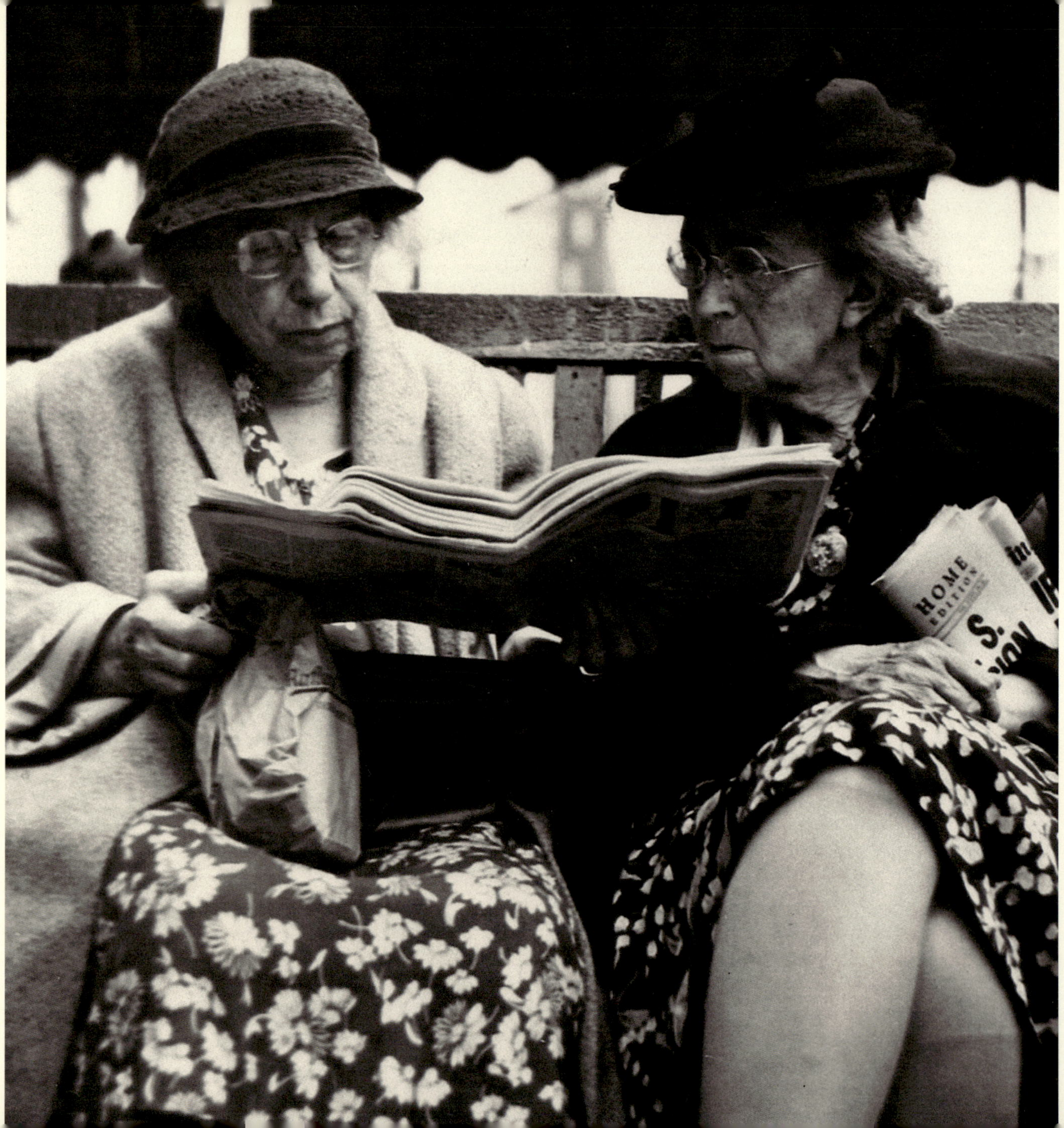

PAGE 26
The Green Benches at St. Petersburg

PAGE 27
Winter Resorters

PAGE 28
Winter Resorters

RIGHT
Sponge Diver's Suit, Tarpon Springs

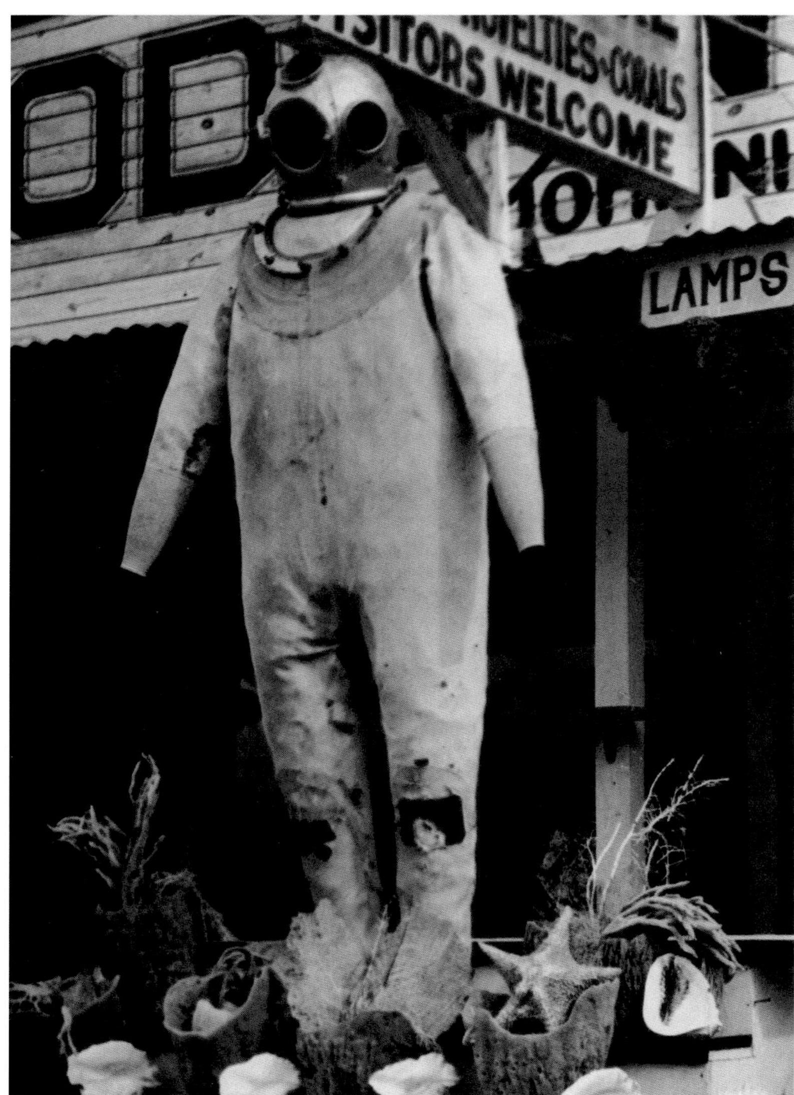

For his Sarasota photographs, Evans managed to capture the things that were unique to the town. First, of course, came the circus. Time after time he journeyed out to the east of town to visit the Ringling circus winter quarters and photograph the animals, the architecture, the railroad cars, and most of all, the elaborate, hand-carved circus wagons that were used in countless parades down the Main Streets of countless American towns.

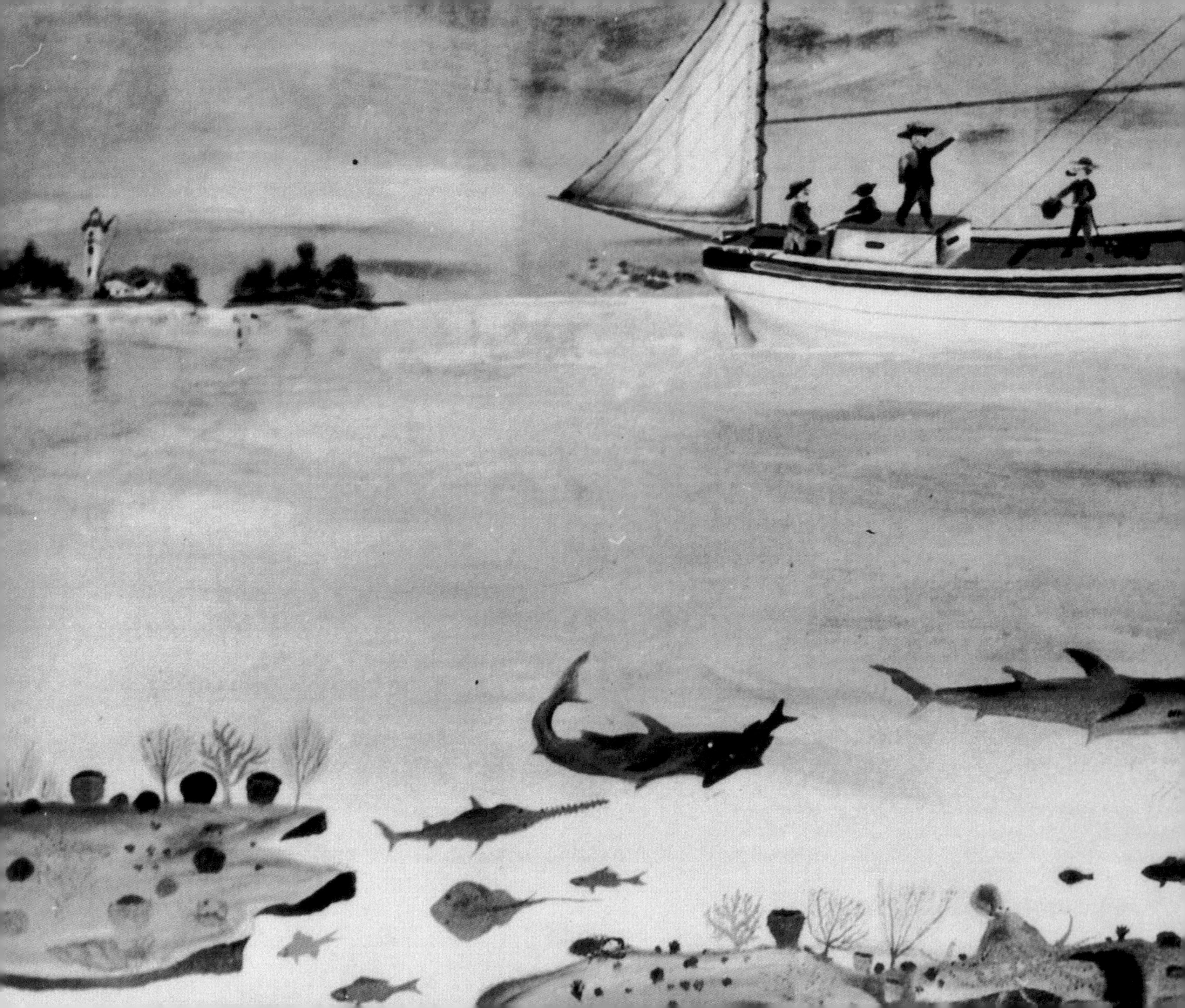

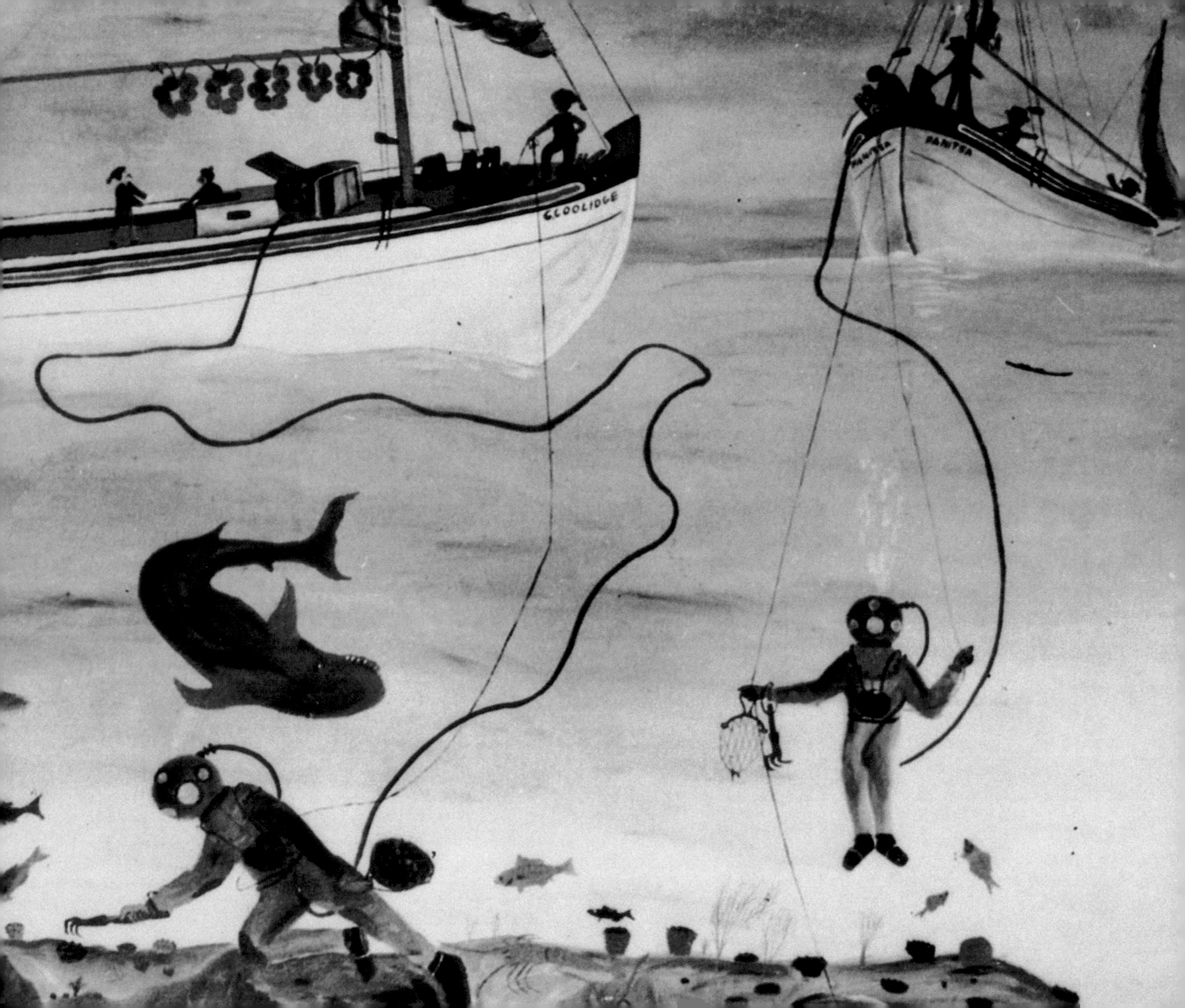
CCOOLIDGE

PAGES 30—31
Descriptive Painting by a Sponge Diver

RIGHT
Caged Baboon, Circus Winter Quarters

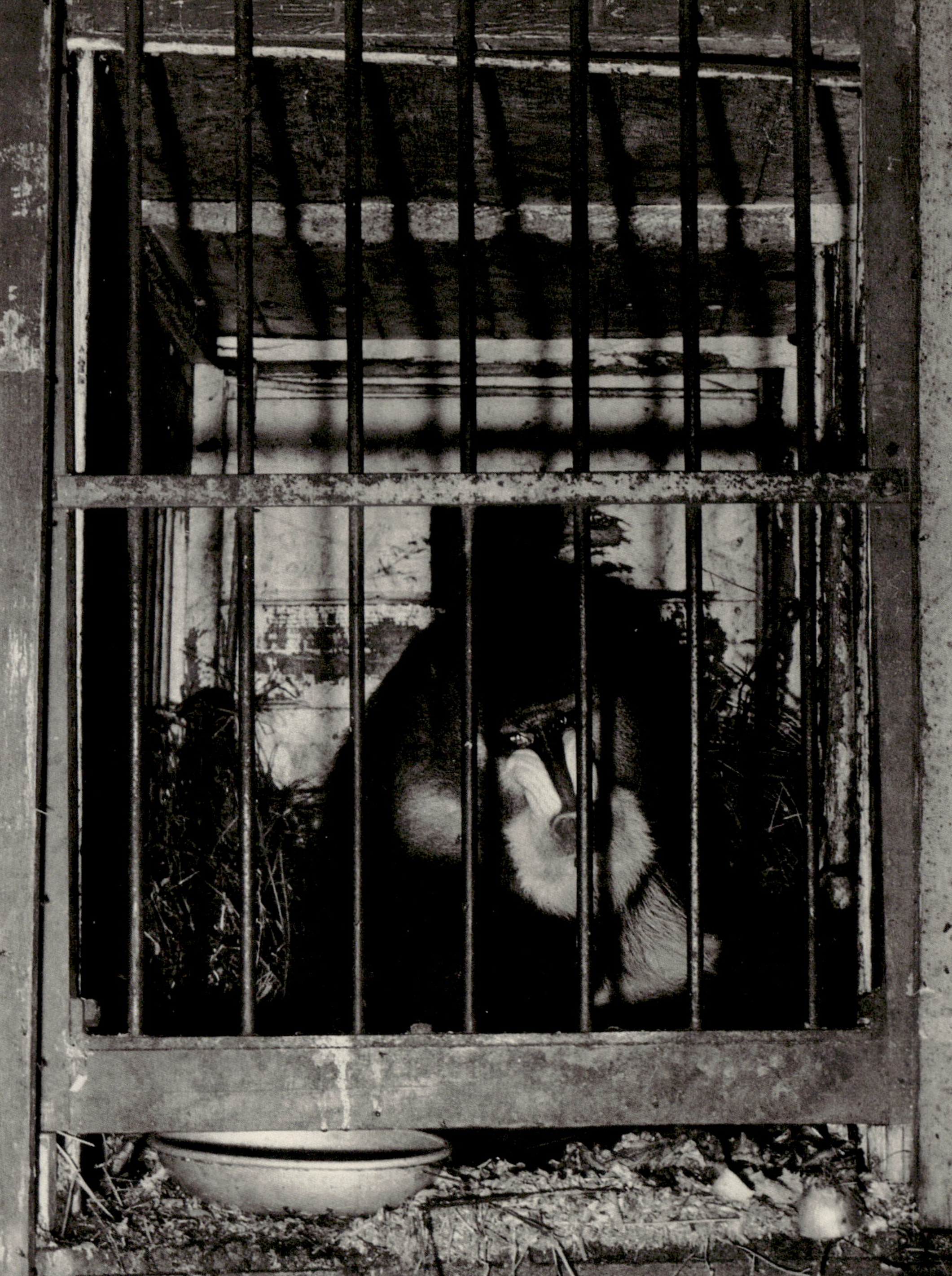

The twentieth century has killed off many things, but its saddest casualty may well be the circus.

It is hard for us to imagine the hold the circus had on everyday life sixty or so years ago. For many children, the day the circus came to town was the high point of the year.

The story of Sarasota and the circus is a sad one, particularly because it began so happily. Back in the 1920s John Ringling, the brains of the five Ringling brothers, came to Sarasota for a vacation. He was immediately struck by the town's potential and began buying up everything in sight, developing it, selling lots, laying out streets; he was, quite literally, building a city.

RIGHT
Balcony Car, Circus Train,
Winter Quarters, Sarasota

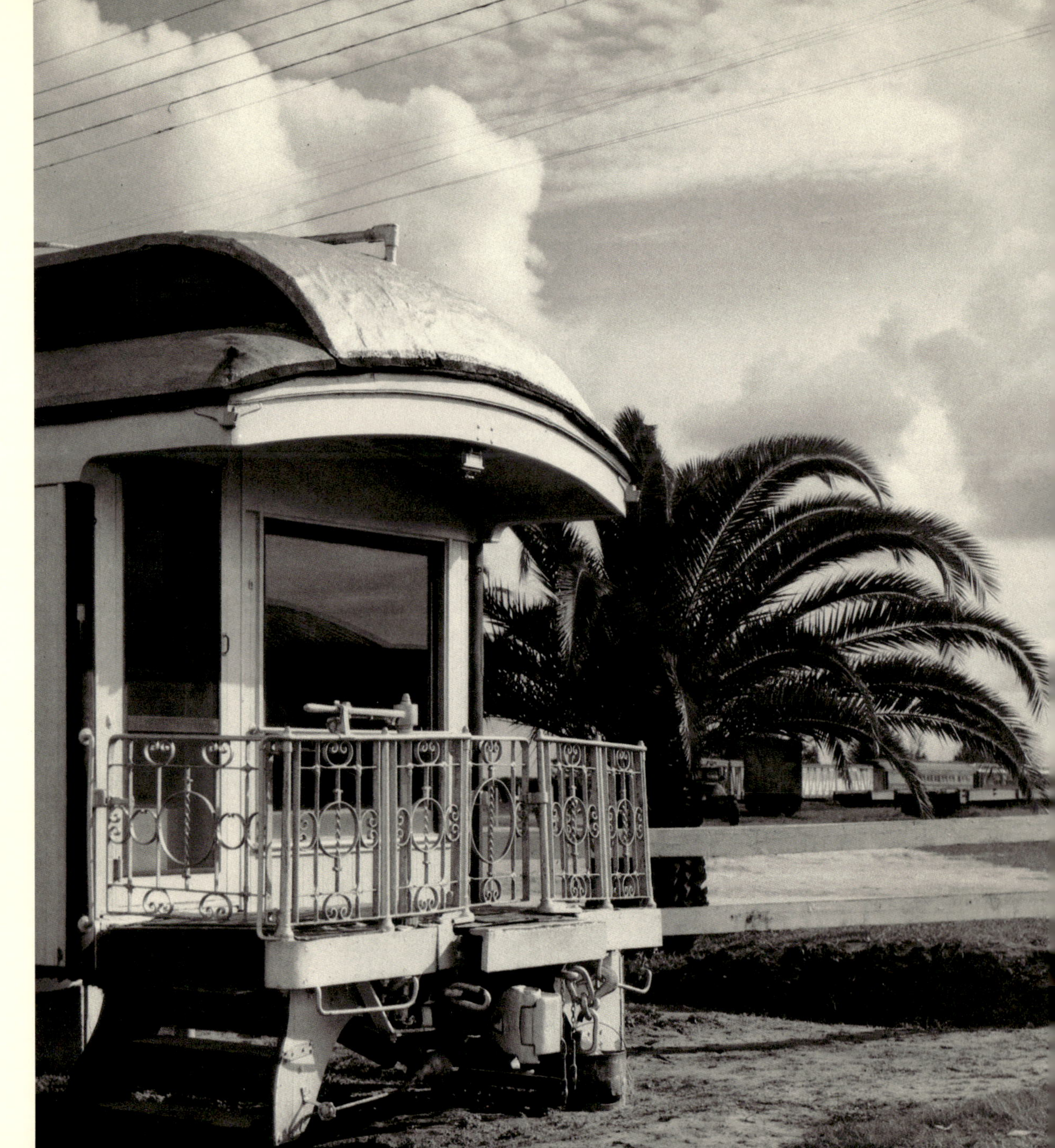

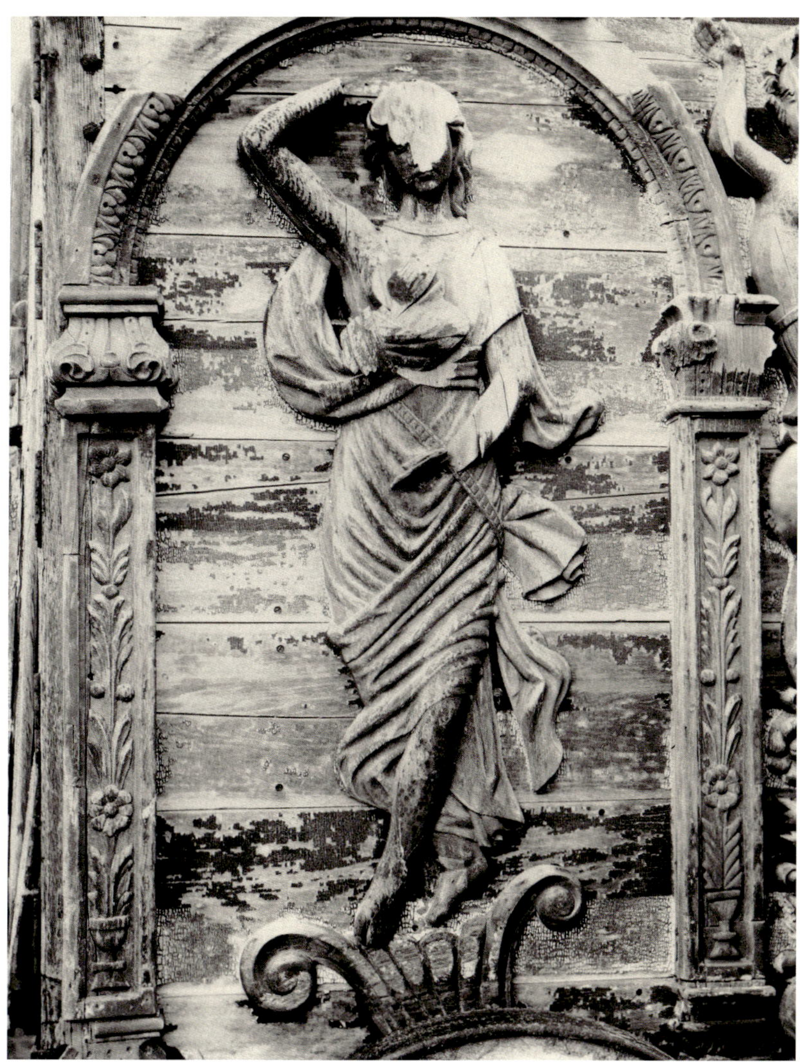

LEFT
Ringling Bandwagon, Circus Winter Quarters, Sarasota

PAGES 36–37
Uninhabited Seaside Residence in Sarasota (Ca'd'Zan, formerly the Ringling Residence)

He constructed a palace on the bay for himself and his wife Mable and his collection of Old Masters and began work on a Ritz Carlton Hotel. In 1927 he moved his entire operation here from Bridgeport, Connecticut (where, interestingly, Walker Evans also took photographs in the '40s—but that's another story). Sarasota suddenly became unique in the world: it was a one-industry town, and that industry was the circus.

For years it was a role that Sarasota played proudly. In no time the winter quarters, with its menagerie and rehearsals open to the public in an outdoor arena built to the exact specifications of Madison Square Garden, became the biggest tourist attraction in the state. It was the Disney World of its day. Tourists still show up looking for it. And when the depression hit, the circus enabled the town to survive quite nicely. The performers put down roots here, as much as circus performers can, and for a small town in Florida, Sarasota developed quite an eclectic population mix. We had aerialists from Europe; we had midgets—for a time we had more ex-Munchkins than any place in the world; I used to see them in the supermarket, but sadly most have passed away. And we had the Ringlings themselves, with their mansions on the bay and their *Dynasty*-like struggles over control of their empire.

When Evans visited in 1941 the circus was still in its glory days, and glorious they were. One small example: the elephants he photographed going through their paces in the outdoor arena would, in a matter of weeks, begin work on their new showstopper for the 1942 season. It was a "Circus Polka" with music commissioned especially from Igor Stravinsky, to be choreographed by George Balanchine, with costumes by Norman Bel Geddes.

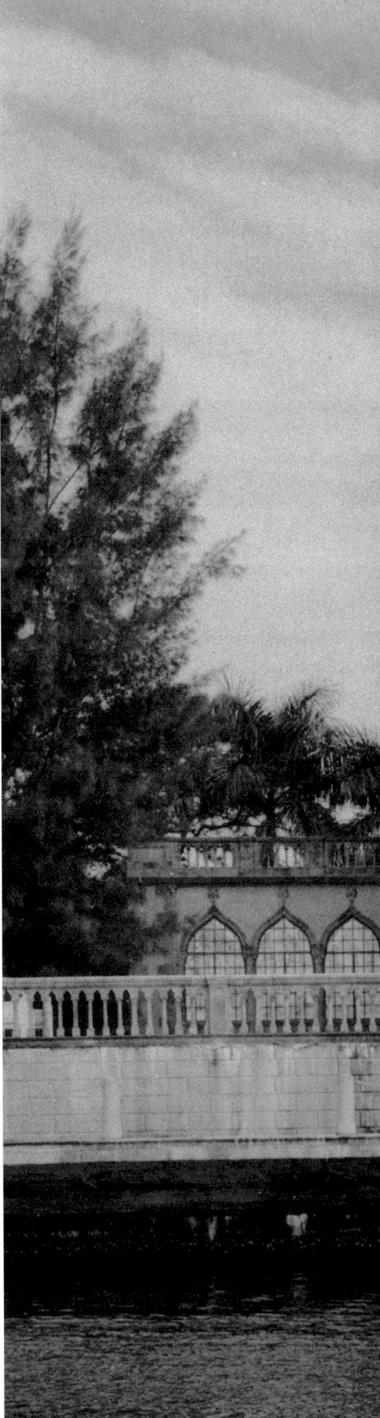

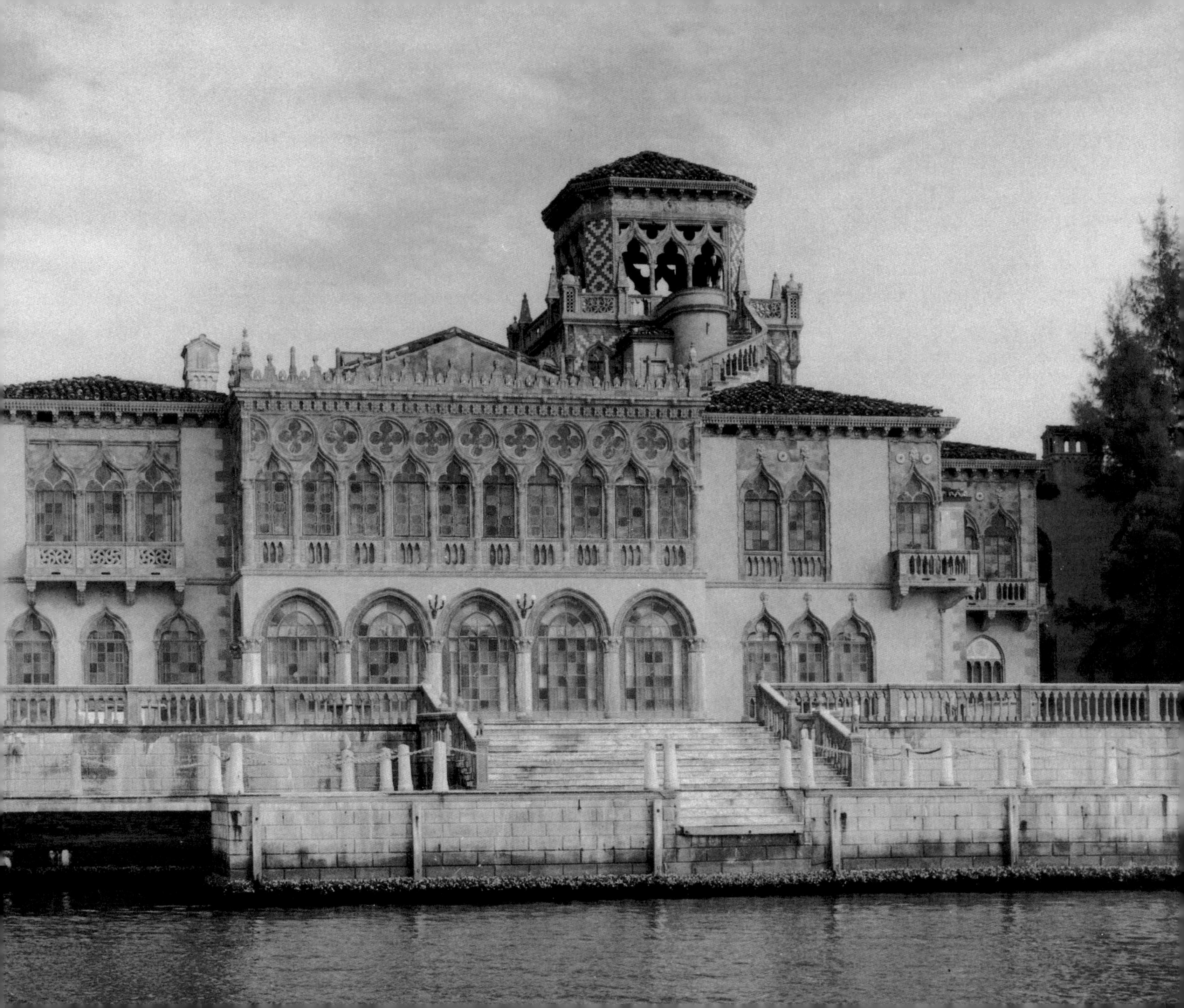

BELOW
Unfinished Boomtime Hotel

OPPOSITE
Circus Trainer with Performing Elephant, Winter Quarters, Sarasota

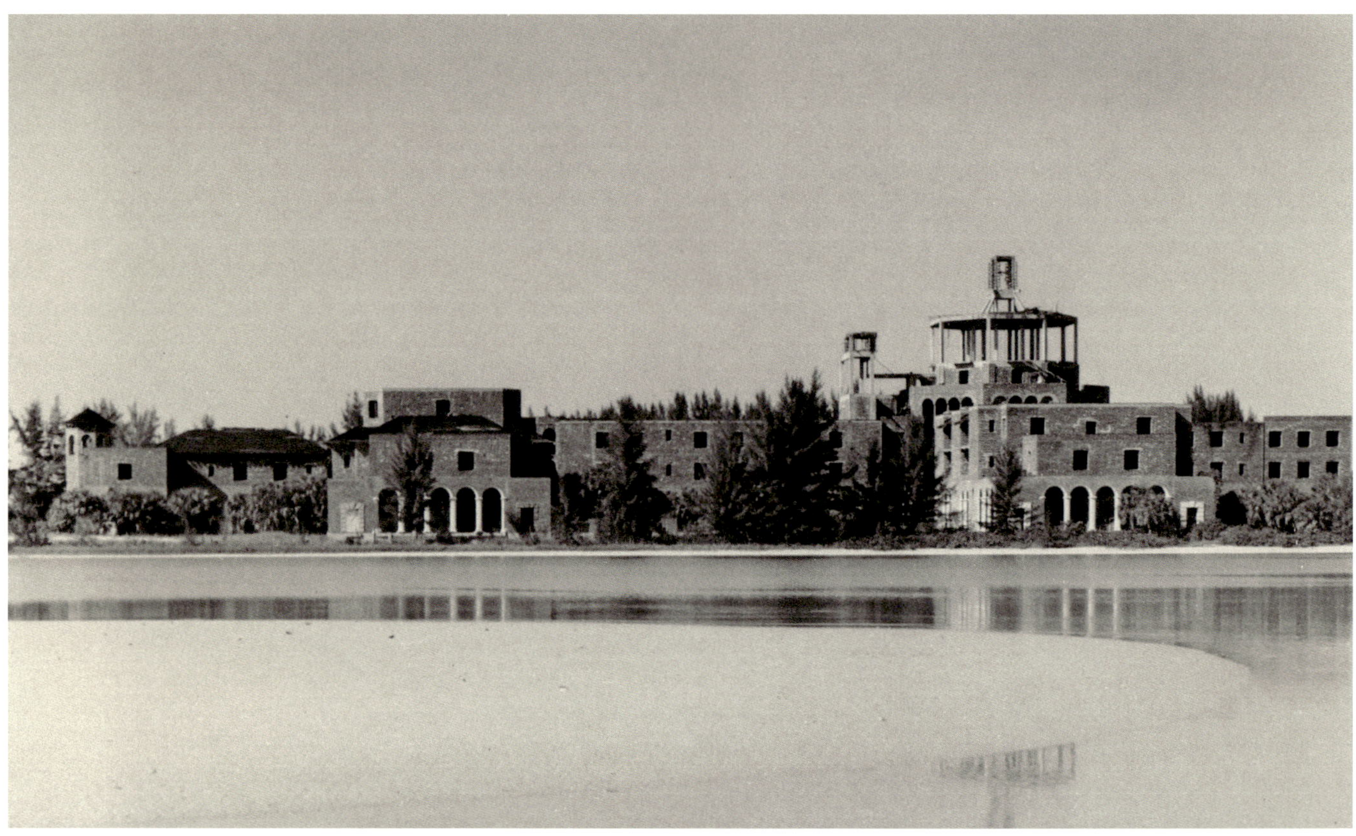

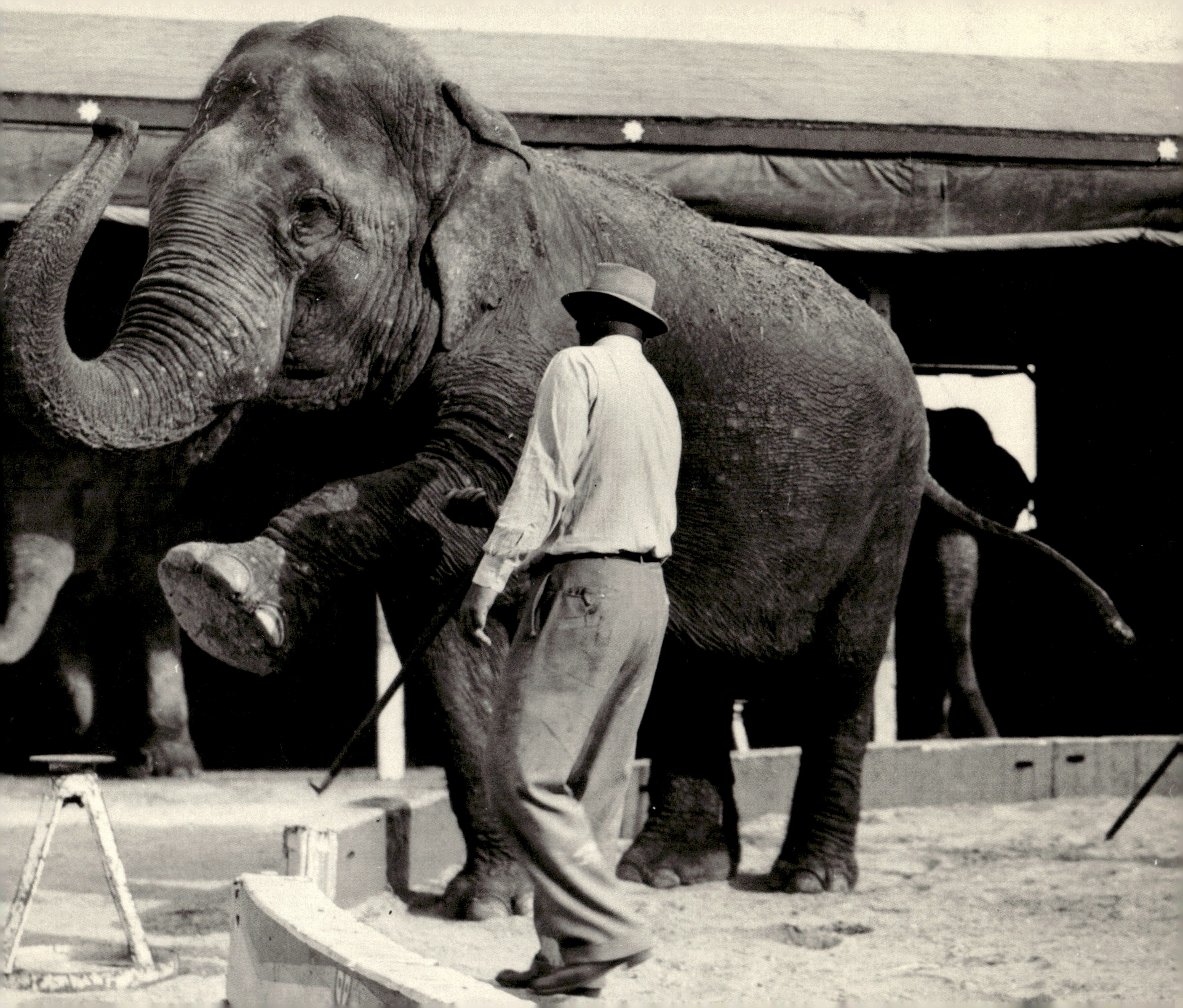

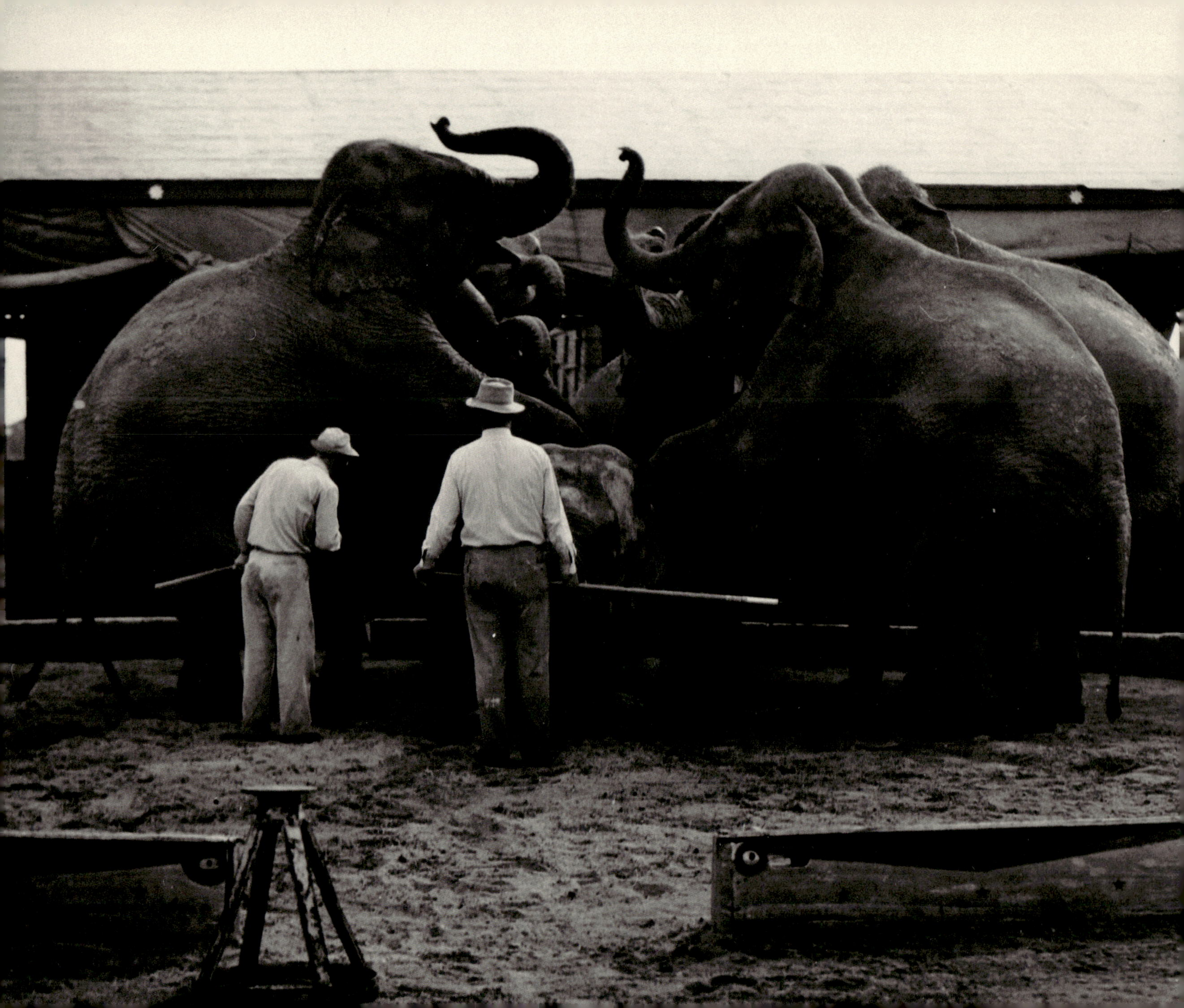

The stars were Old Modoc, the great circus elephant buried somewhere in an unmarked grave in the Kensington Park subdivision, and Vera Zorina, who was then Balanchine's wife. The *New York Times* (April 10, 1942) pronounced it "breathtaking":

> The cast included fifty ballet girls, all in fluffy pink, and fifty dancing elephants. They came into the ring in artificial, blue-lighted dusk, first the little pink dancers, then the great beasts. The little dancers pirouetted into the three rings and the elephant herds gravely swayed and nodded rhythmically. The arc of sway widened and the stomping picked up with the music. In the central ring Modoc the Elephant danced with amazing grace, and in time to the tune, closing in perfect cadence with the crashing finale. In the last dance fifty elephants moved in an endless chain around the great ring, trunk to tail, with the little pink ballet girls in the blue twilight behind them. The ground shook with the elephants' measured steps.

OPPOSITE
Two Circus Trainers with Performing Elephants, Winter Quarters, Sarasota

PAGE 42
Three Circus Train Cars, Winter Quarters, Sarasota

Television killed the circus. But Sarasota, to its shame, helped out.

Just when things were getting really bad and the circus needed every break it could get, Sarasota ungratefully zoned it out of town. It seems that circus people live with an inordinate amount of strange equipment—gaudy trailers, wild animals, trapeze rigging in the backyard—and one by one all these necessities were prohibited. They had become a little embarrassing in a carnival, honky-tonk sort of way. Besides, the town had found a new source of wealth: the retired Midwesterners who began moving here in the 1950s.

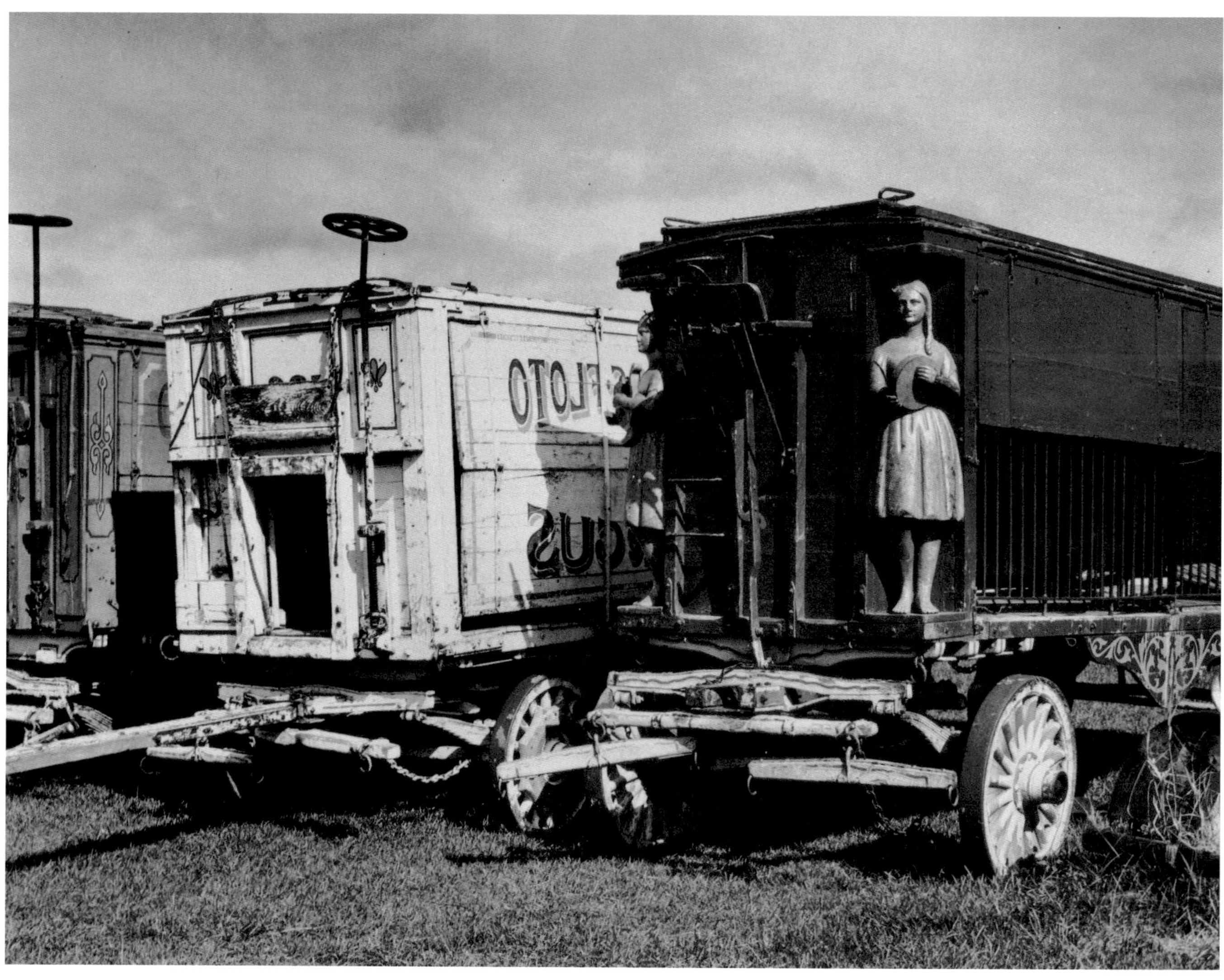

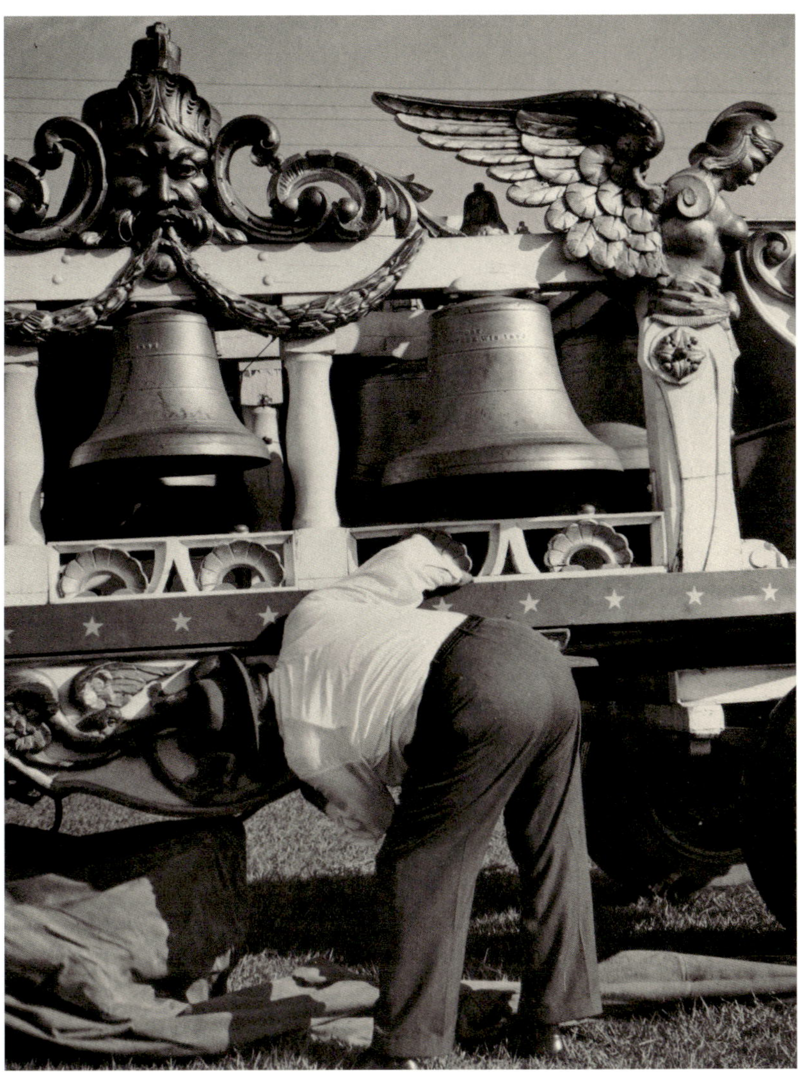

Even though Ringling Bros. left in 1960, first moving to Venice, then to Tampa, Sarasota remains a circus town. Over a dozen smaller circuses are headquartered here, though their performance schedules get smaller and smaller with each passing year. Many of the great circus families are still here, though most of the younger members have left the business. My old neighbor Gunther Wallenda taught history at Sarasota High. And Olympia Zacchini, the daughter of the first woman shot out of a cannon, is a prominent local artist. There is one Ringling left in town, Pat Ringling Buck. She is a gossip columnist just like me. Or she was. Now she's a critic.

PAGE 43
Man at Work on Circus Wagon, Sarasota

RIGHT
Detail of Circus Wagon, Sarasota

OPPOSITE
Circus Winter Quarters, Sarasota

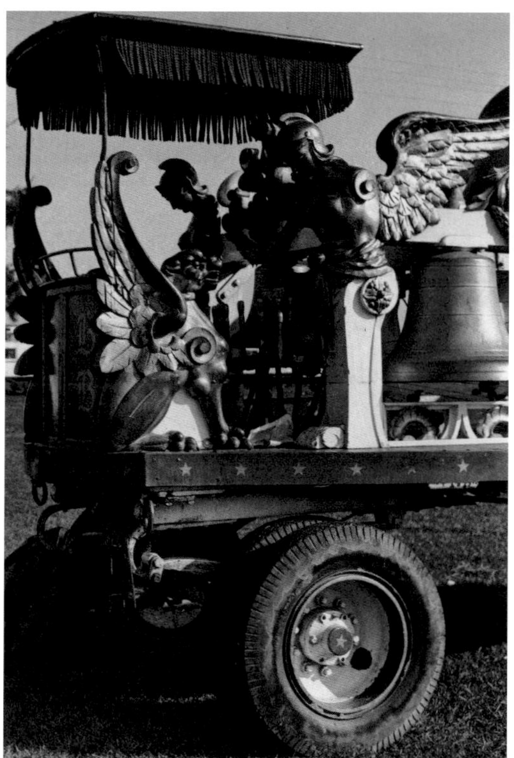

But if the circus is but a shell of its former self, it has given Sarasota a history of creative endeavor unparalleled in the world. This is the town where the famous gag with all the clowns piling out of the tiny car was invented. This is where Franz Unus lived, the man who could stand on one finger. And then there were the elephants. What the *New York Times* didn't tell you about was an incident that occurred during a rehearsal at the winter quarters. Things were going fine until a sudden noise frightened the herd and they all took off en masse, heading south. The image of a distraught George Balanchine chasing a herd of elephants, all clad in pink tutus, down Lockwood Ridge Road—that, to me, is Sarasota, and always will be.

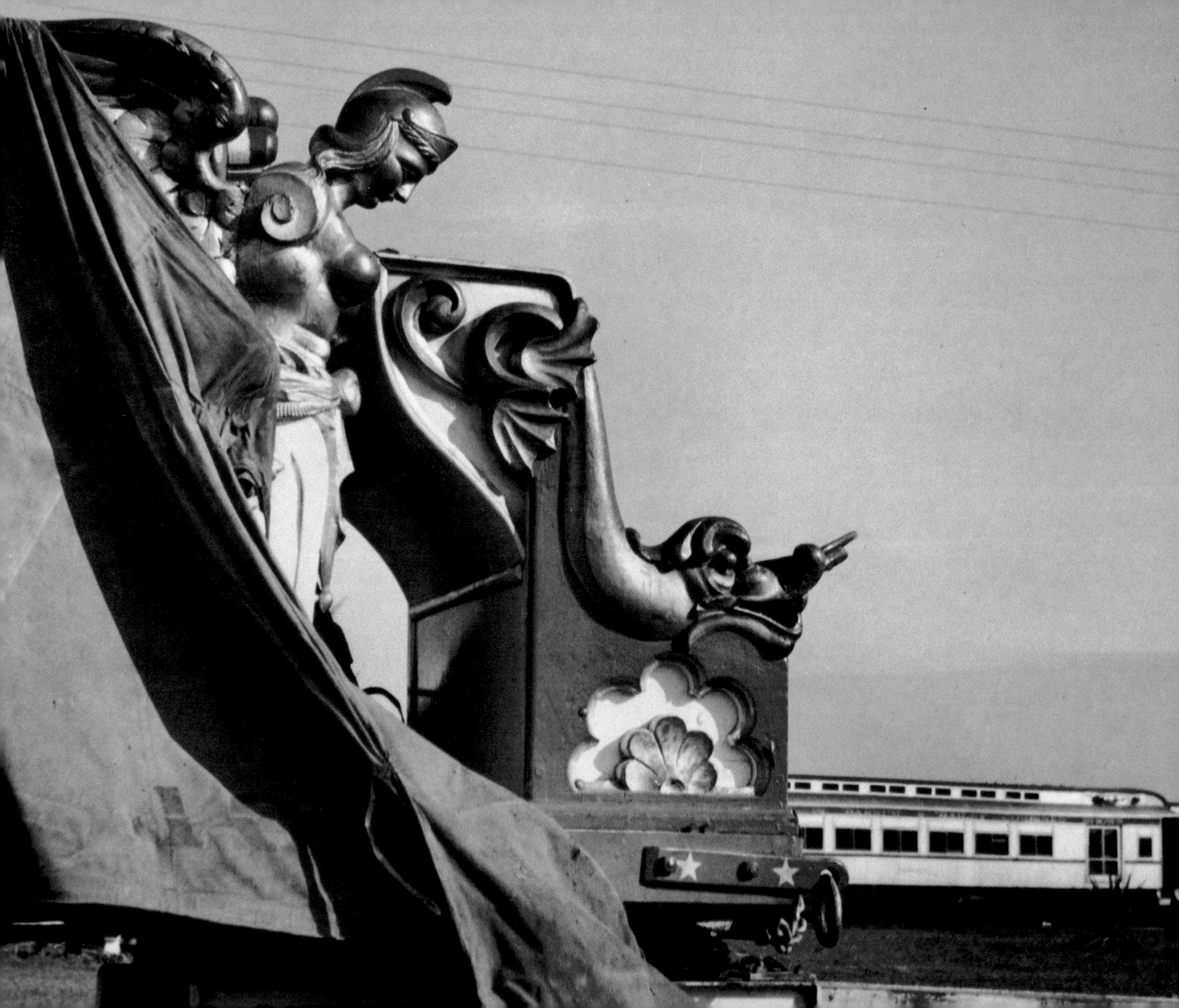

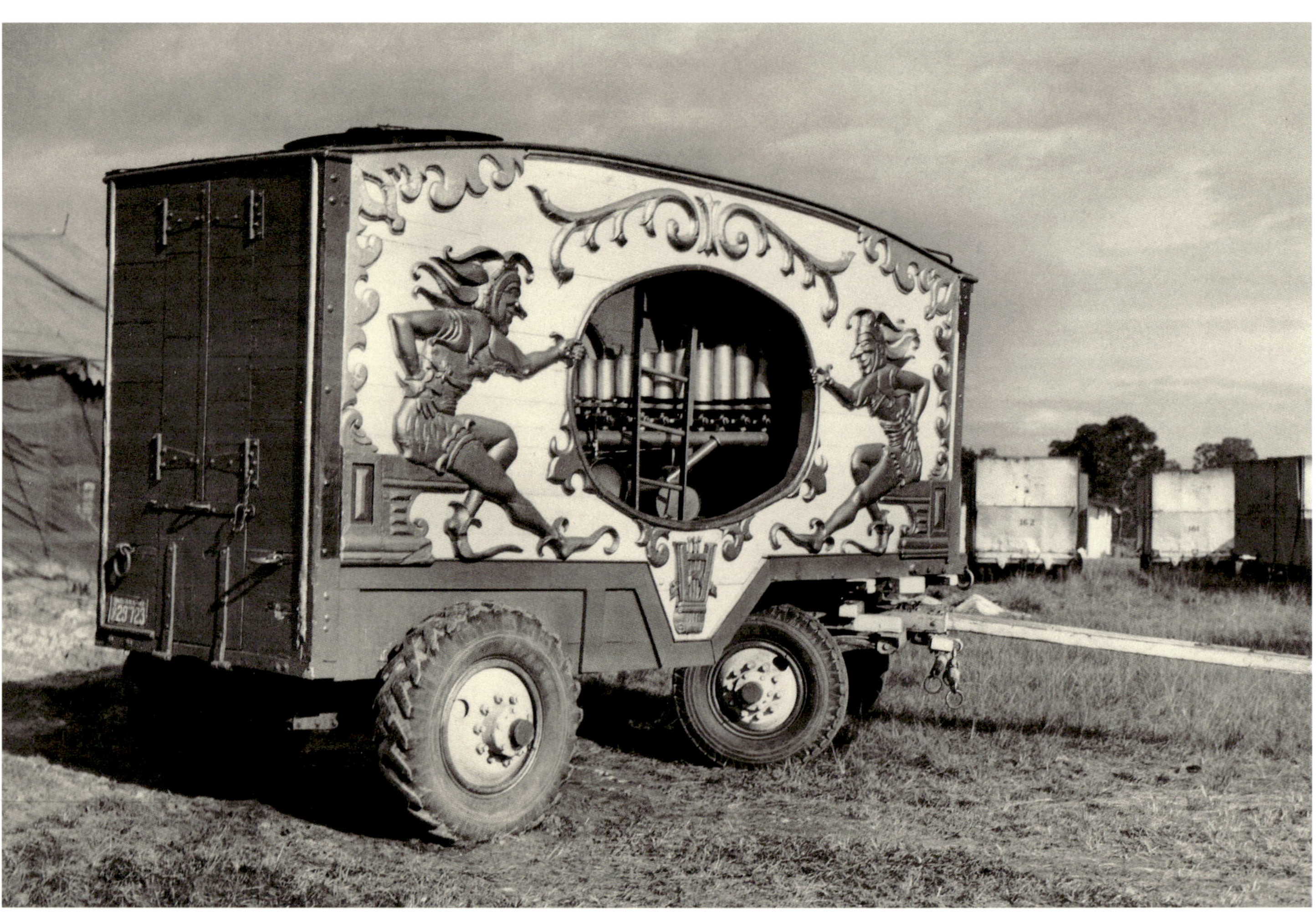

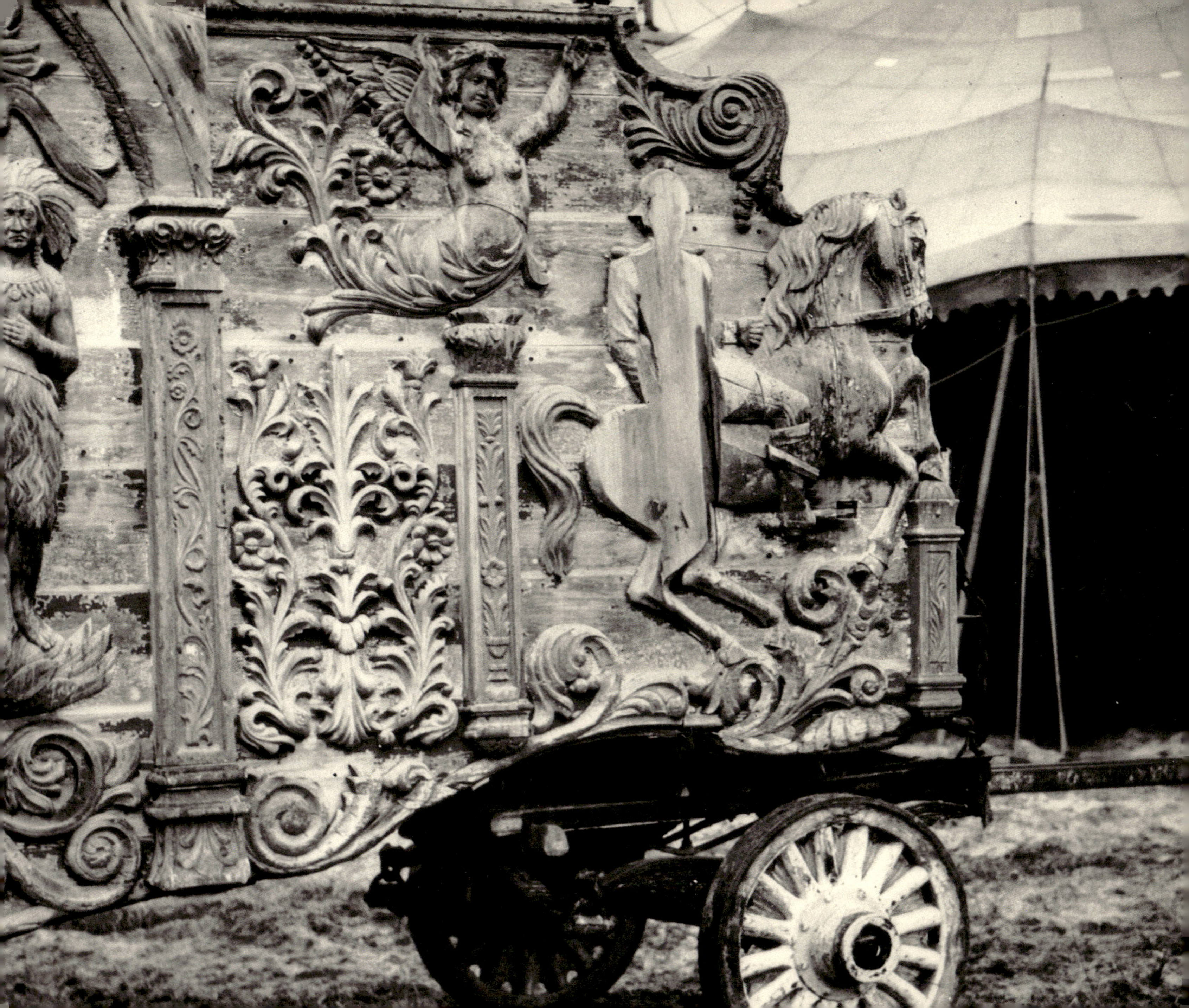

PAGE 46
Circus Wagon (Calliope Car), Winter Quarters, Sarasota

PAGE 47
Ringling Bandwagon, Circus Winter Quarters, Sarasota

A friend of mine, visiting Sarasota for the first time, called it "pretty, but not *that* pretty." It is flat as a board. The vegetation is scrubby in some areas, tropical in others. There is nothing dramatic or breathtaking about it; when real beauty takes over, it comes from the changing colors of the sky and water.

This was something Walker Evans was not much interested in. He was clearly an artist who did not fall victim to nature's charms. No wonder Ansel Adams hated his work. The only natural thing he really liked was driftwood, which at least he could collect. One can even sense a certain hostility in his photographs of the Mangrove Coast's

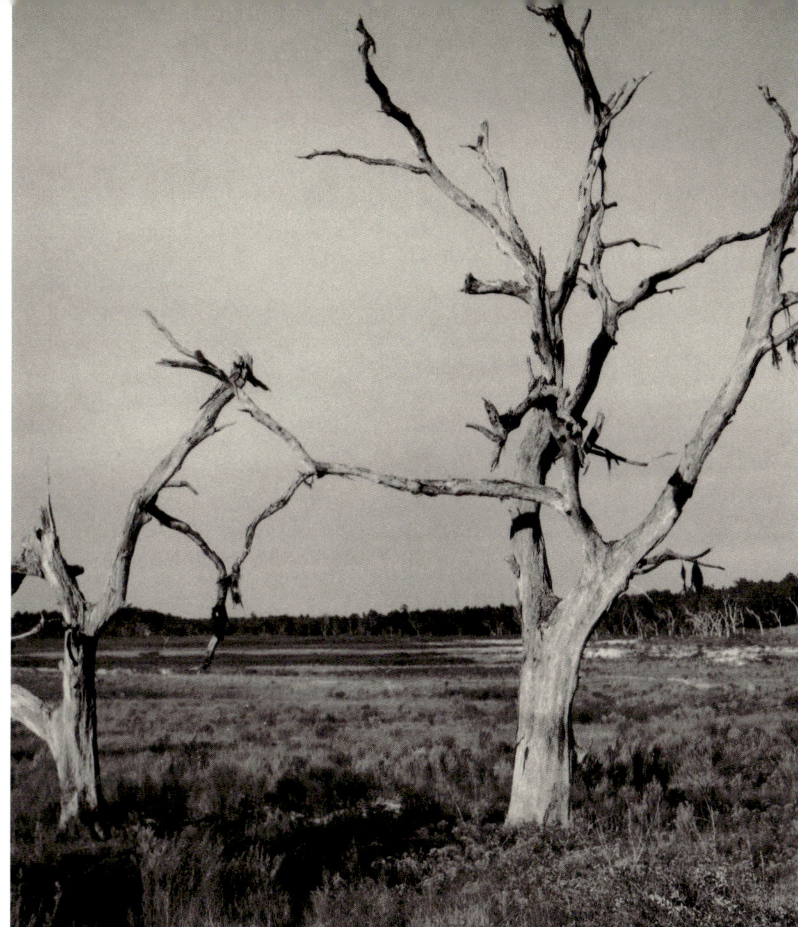

LEFT
Inland Landscape

BELOW
Pelican on a Dock

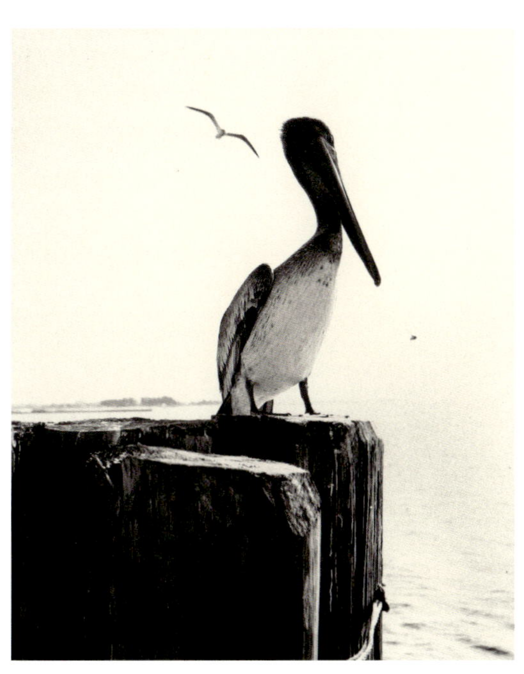

beaches and swamps. The swamps I can understand; back in those days they were not revered as fragile ecosystems, they were the enemy—useless for any purpose whatsoever and full of dangerous things like alligators. Many Floridians still look upon them this way, and not without reason. Alligators, reveling in a big comeback from their endangered-species status, are making off with children and small dogs at an alarming rate. At one retirement community they have a volunteer alligator patrol during poodle-walking hours.

The world is a poorer place for not having a Walker Evans photograph of a live alligator; they were his kind of animal. Instead, he fell for the pelican. If you live here for any length of time, the pelican becomes about as interesting as the squirrel. Seabirds have a downside—they are vicious, stubborn, and greedy. They are always getting caught in hooks and fishing lines and then being rushed to the Pelican Man's Bird Sanctuary, one of the town's more popular charities.

I can forgive the swamps. I can forgive the pelicans, who do, after all, mate for life. But I really wish he had tried a little harder with the beaches. They are, after all, our bread and butter. One of them even won a Best Sand in the World contest. They can hold their own with any resort in the world.

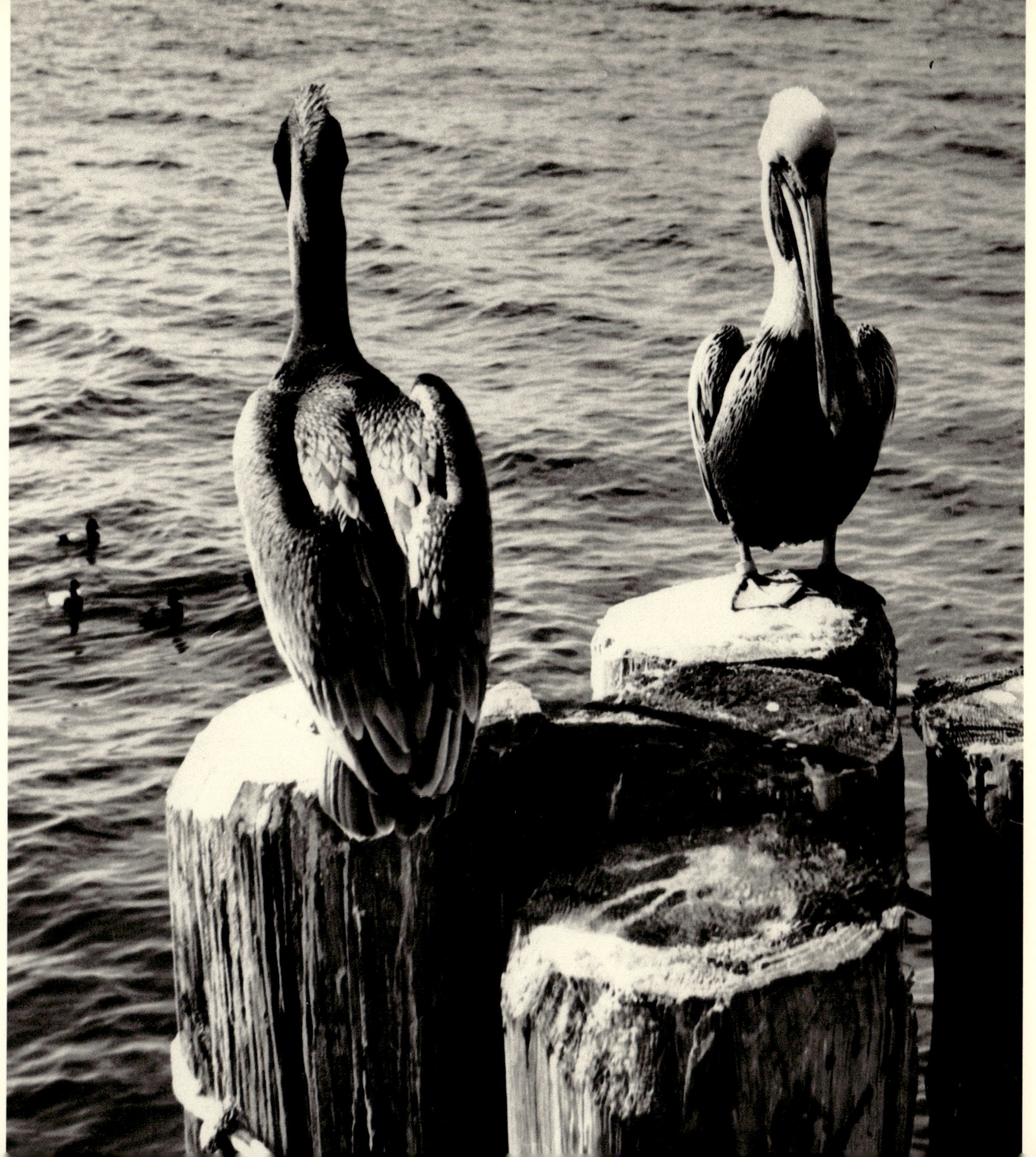

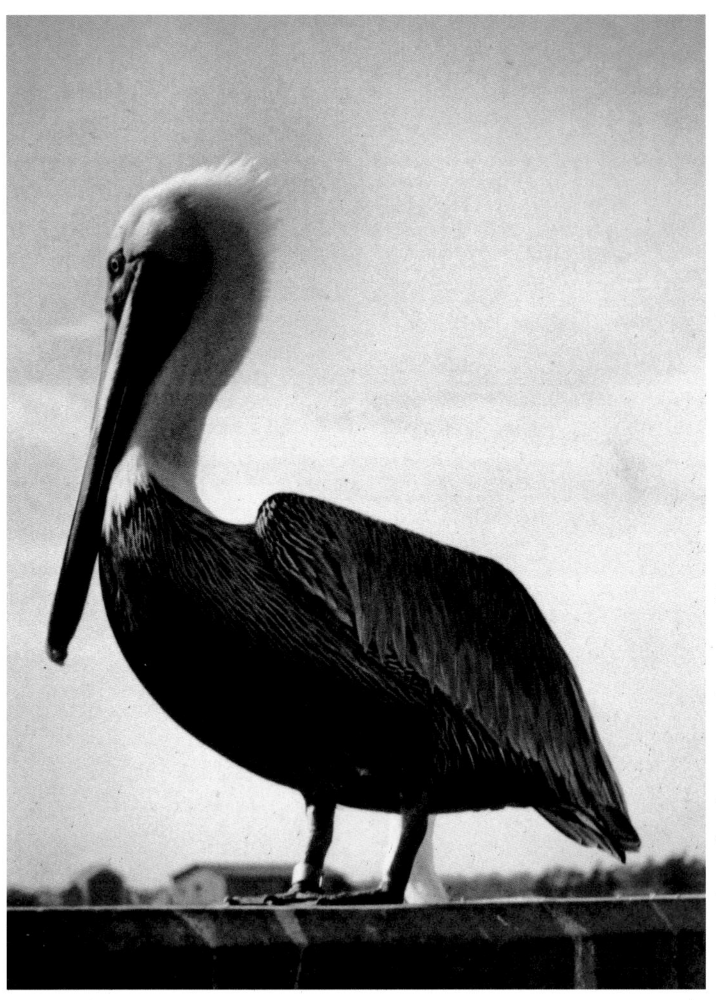

True, the water does tend to be a little tepid and calm and bathtub-like, particularly in August, and they are eroding at an appalling rate. But they remain the town's pride and joy, not to mention a little gold mine.

But where are they? All we get are several shots of misshapen palm trees growing much too close to the waterline. Where is the Lido Casino, the glorious Art Deco beach pavilion championed by his host, Mr. Bickel, but sadly torn down in the 1960s? Where are the pale tourists, the tots with pails, the shell collectors?

Apparently Evans just wasn't a beach person.

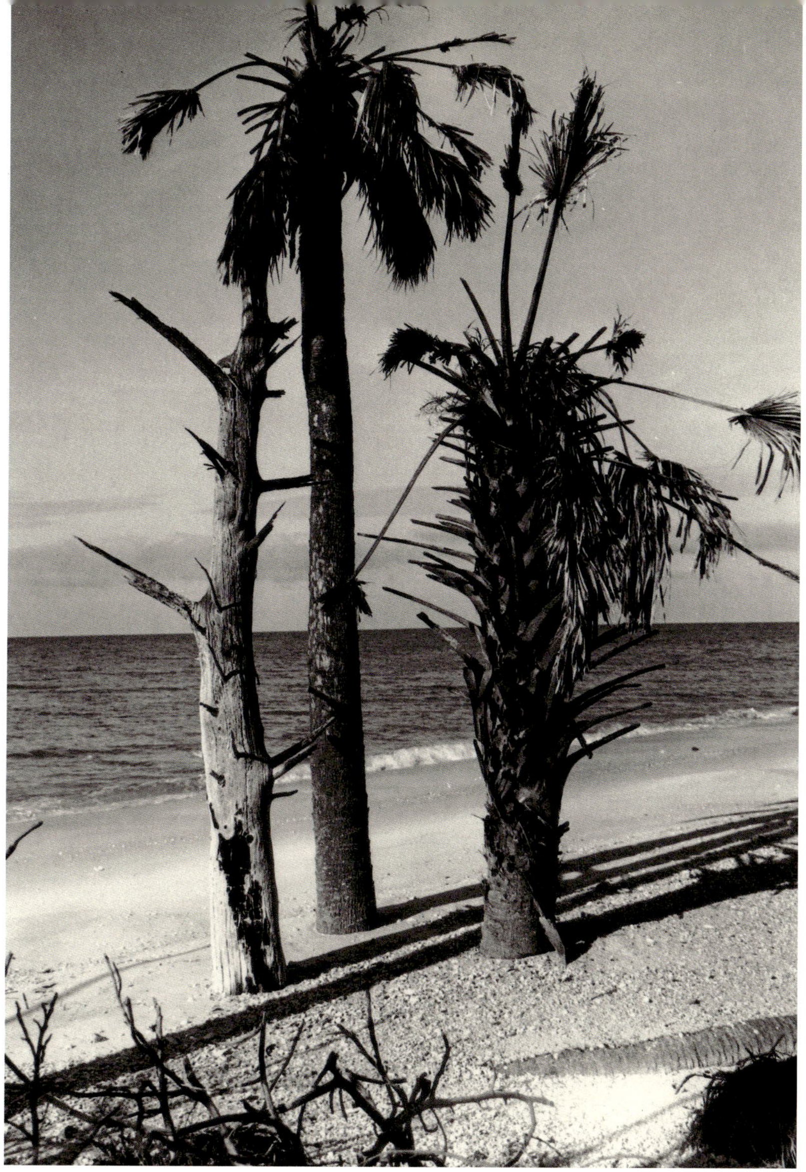

PAGE 51
Two Pelicans on a Dock

OPPOSITE
Pelican

LEFT
Three Palms

BELOW
Gulf of Mexico

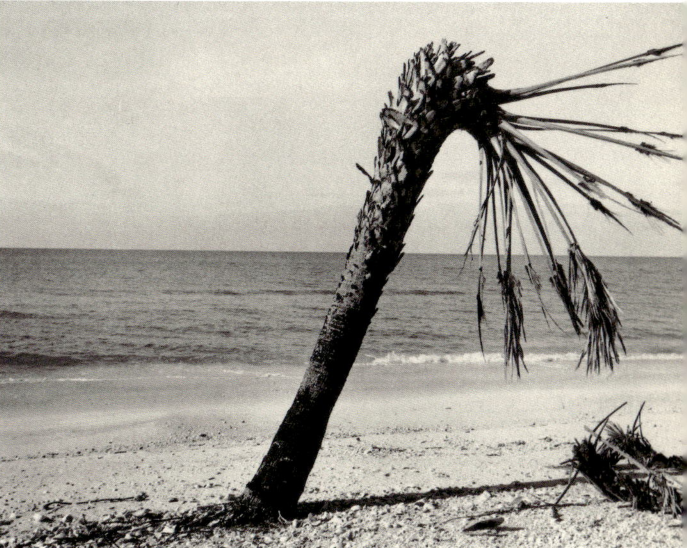

But if he didn't like the beach, he certainly liked trailers.

I've yet to meet another person whose enthusiasm for trailers matches mine, but I think that Evans may well be that person, my imaginary trailer friend, so to speak.

For years I've been trying to get people to pay attention to these fascinating things, but it's clear that they are just not going to. That's one of the reasons it's so hard to do research about trailers. There's been nothing written about them. And it doesn't look like the situation is about to change. I've been shopping around my coffee-table book, *Trailer Style,* for years, without a nibble. People just don't get it.

But I have the feeling that they were right up Evans's alley. Imagine: a little metal house that moves. How could you *not* be fascinated?

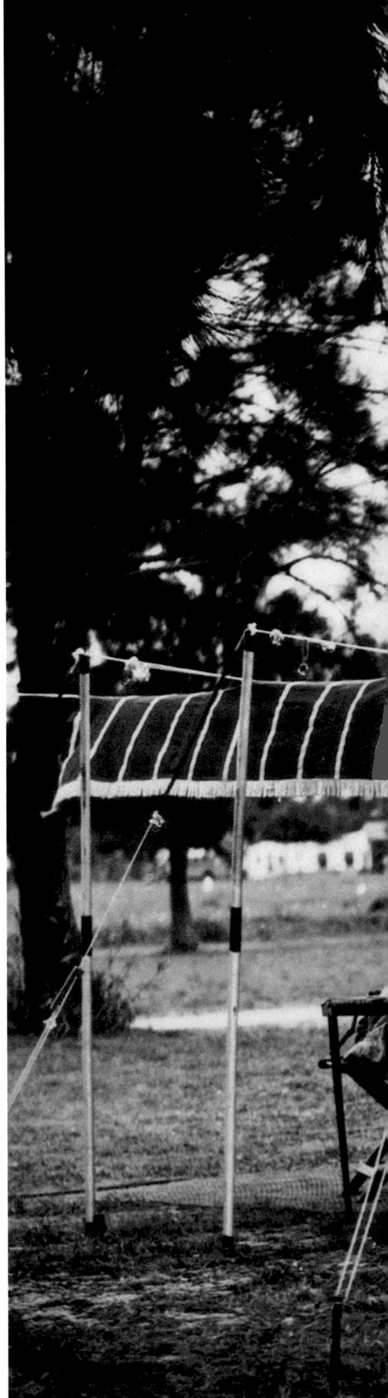

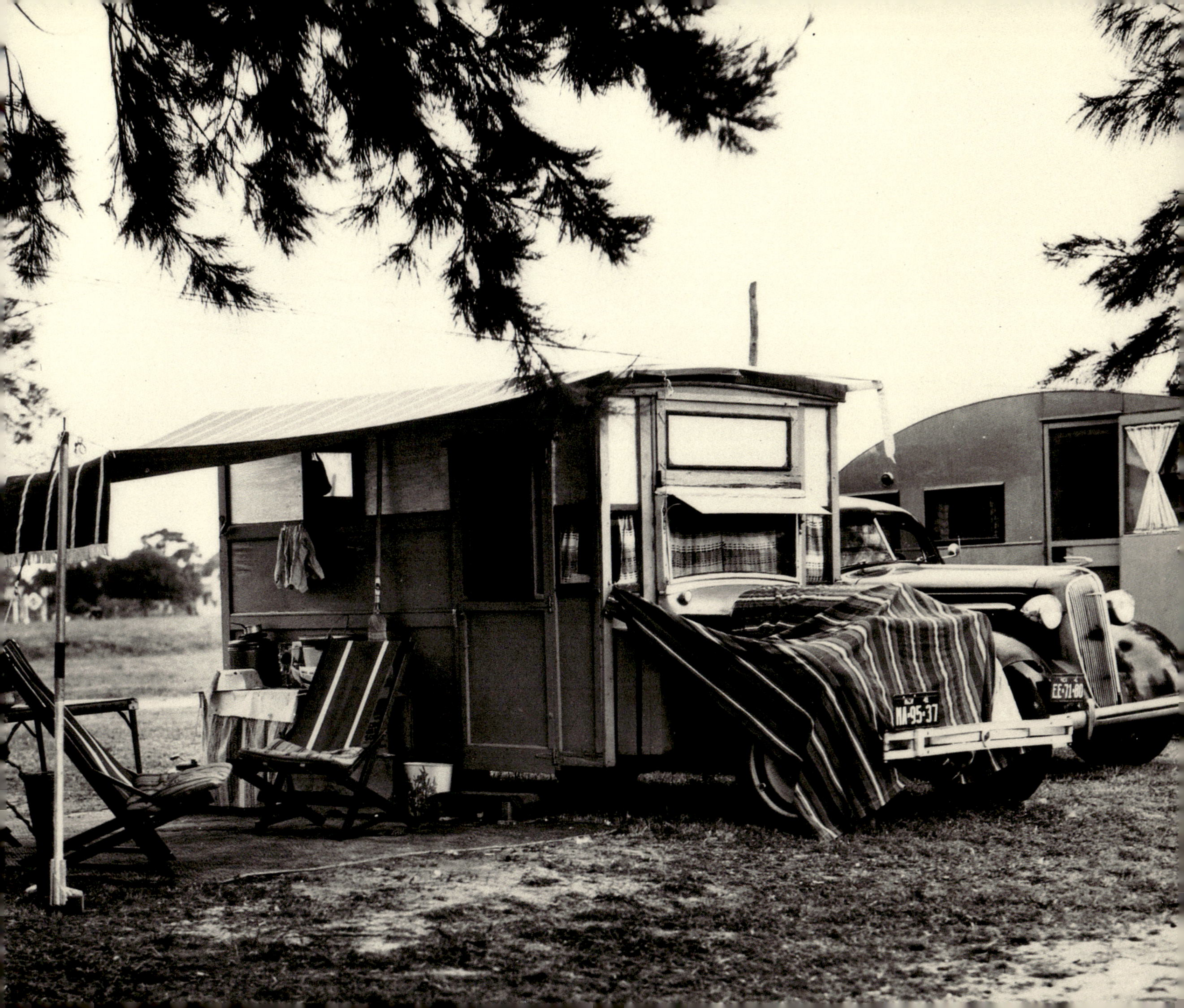

MA-95-37
EE-71-80

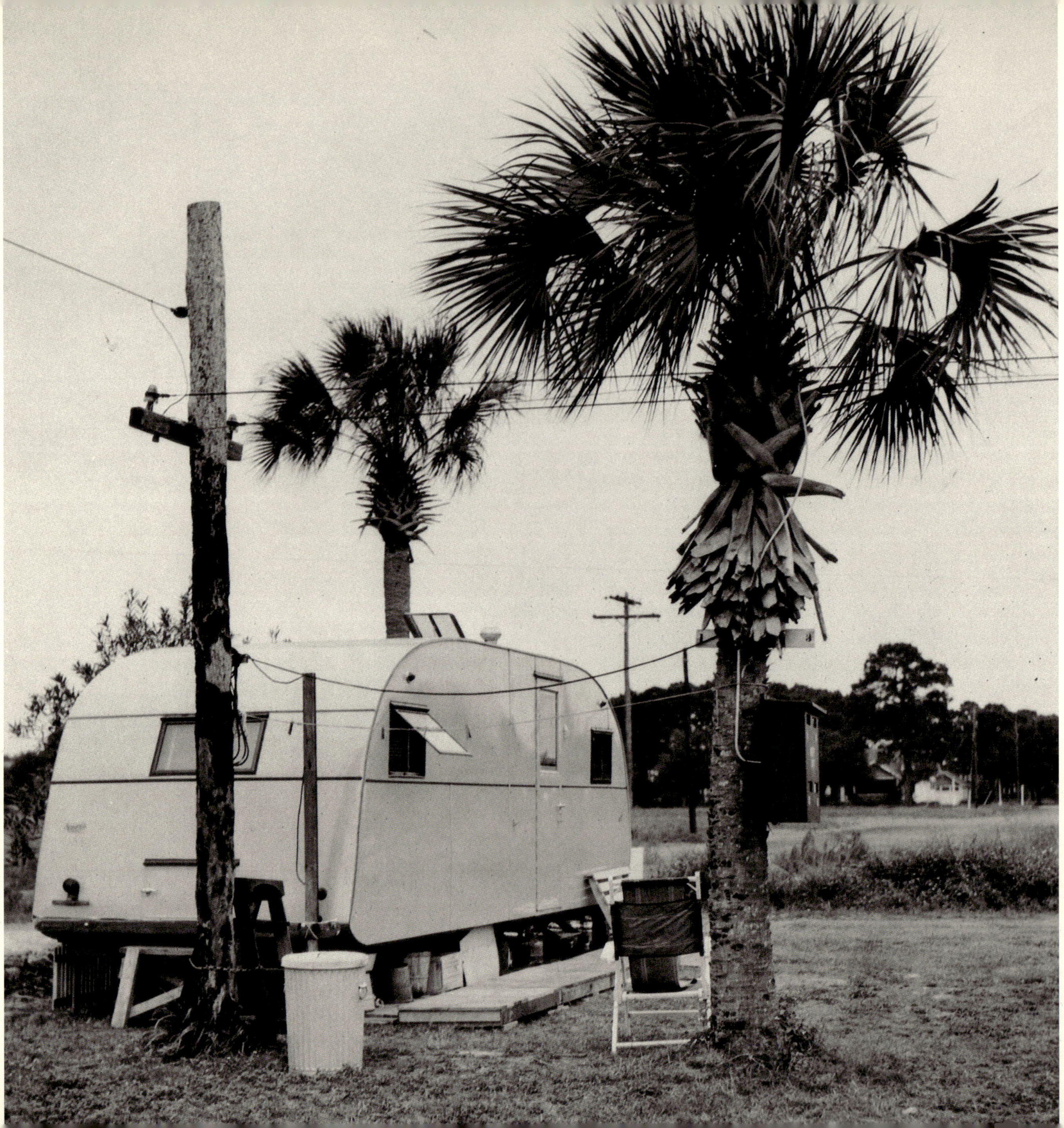

How I would love to show Evans a few of my favorite trailer parks: places like Mel-Mar Village up in Bradenton. Here the trailers are in what I call the "Toaster Style," which clearly caught Evans's eye, too [opposite page]. Everywhere you look there are long-forgotten names: First Lady, Pine Tree, Pal, Flame, and New Moon. Clearly Mel-Mar Village belongs to the Classic Period.

Or rather the Early Classic Period. Windmill Village North—not to be confused with Windmill Village South—is Late Classic. Here the look is 1959. The shape is larger, squarer. Gone is any pretense that these things can move. Porches sprout, plus carports. Bay windows appear, and if you're lucky, you may even get fins.

And yes, there is a windmill. It towers over the place, housing the clubhouse in its base, with the pool right in front. And the streets are named after Dutch cheeses. A good dose of well-done kitsch is always a plus in a trailer park; no one knew this better than Evans.

Recently, when I was in-between houses and had no place to live, I actually got to spend three weeks in such a park. It was called Tropical Acres, and it was heaven. My trailer was a great big double-wide, with so much space that it had rooms I never even went in. (The only problem was a certain wobble when you walked from one end to the other.) My neighbors were the nicest people in the world. When my cat got lost they organized into teams and combed the park, looking under every trailer and even searching the sewage treatment plant next door. My favorite neighbor was the guy right across the street. His trailer was tiny, barely 8 by 12. He and

PAGES 54–55
Recreational Vehicle with Striped Canopy

OPPOSITE
Trailer in Camp, Sarasota

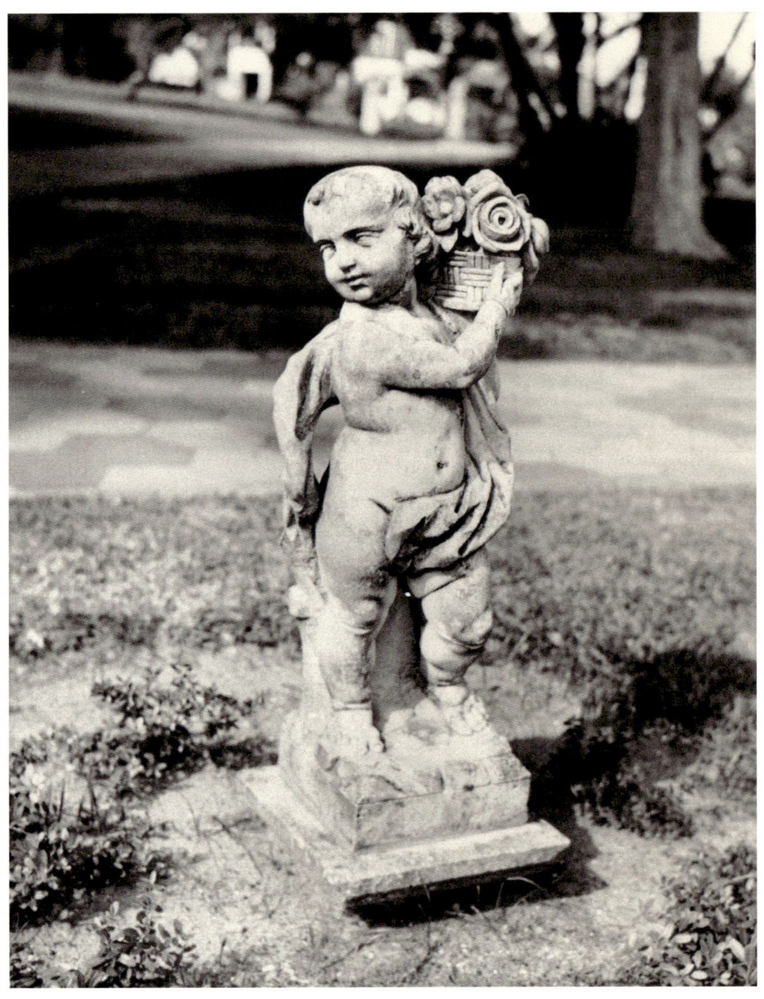

LEFT
Statuette of a Cherub

OPPOSITE
Municipal Trailer Camp

his wife hauled it down each winter from Michigan. In their minuscule front yard they had a plaster goose, and each day they would dress the goose in a different outfit. That goose had more clothes than I did. If it was raining he wore his yellow slicker, but if it was sunny and bright, you never knew what he might have on, and it reached the point where I got out of bed in the morning just to see what the goose might be wearing. My favorite outfit was a gendarme's uniform, complete with a little goose-sized cape. Something tells me Evans would have been very interested in this goose; whenever I think about it, I can almost hear him yelling from beyond the grave: "Get the camera!"

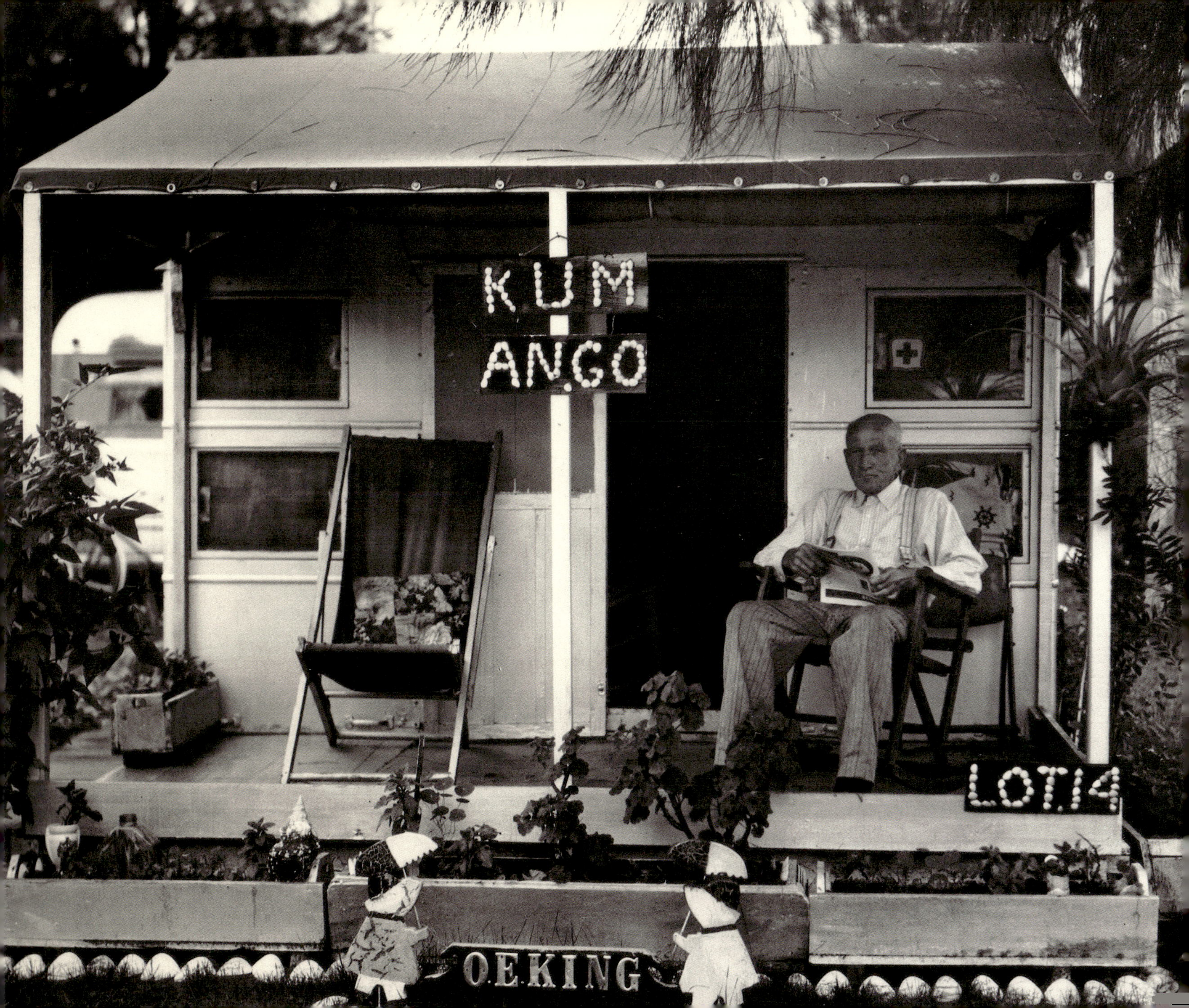
KUM
ANGO
LOT 14
O.E.KING

T*he Mangrove Coast* was published in 1942 and was a big hit—except for the pictures. They just didn't mesh with the text. Bickel was dispensing popular history at its most eager-to-please, full of "lore" about pirates and explorers and moonshiners. The photographs supplied by Evans were about something else entirely. The two sat there in uneasy proximity as the first edition ran its course, but for the second and subsequent editions the photographs were dropped entirely.

I doubt that Evans minded much. Pearl Harbor was attacked while he and Jane were walking on Siesta Beach; from then on, he, like everyone else, had a different set of worries. He went to Washington to investigate war work but ended up becoming a movie critic for *Time*. In 1948 he switched over to the art department at *Fortune*. It was during his tenure that *Fortune* achieved a level of art direction and photography rarely seen in a magazine. It could be argued that his cushy corporate job kept him from his art; in reality, it—like his Sarasota assignment—*became* his art.

Evans would cross paths with the Mangrove Coast again and again. His sister and brother-in-law settled on Anna Maria, the barrier island just north of Longboat, and he would come to visit often, usually to escape the

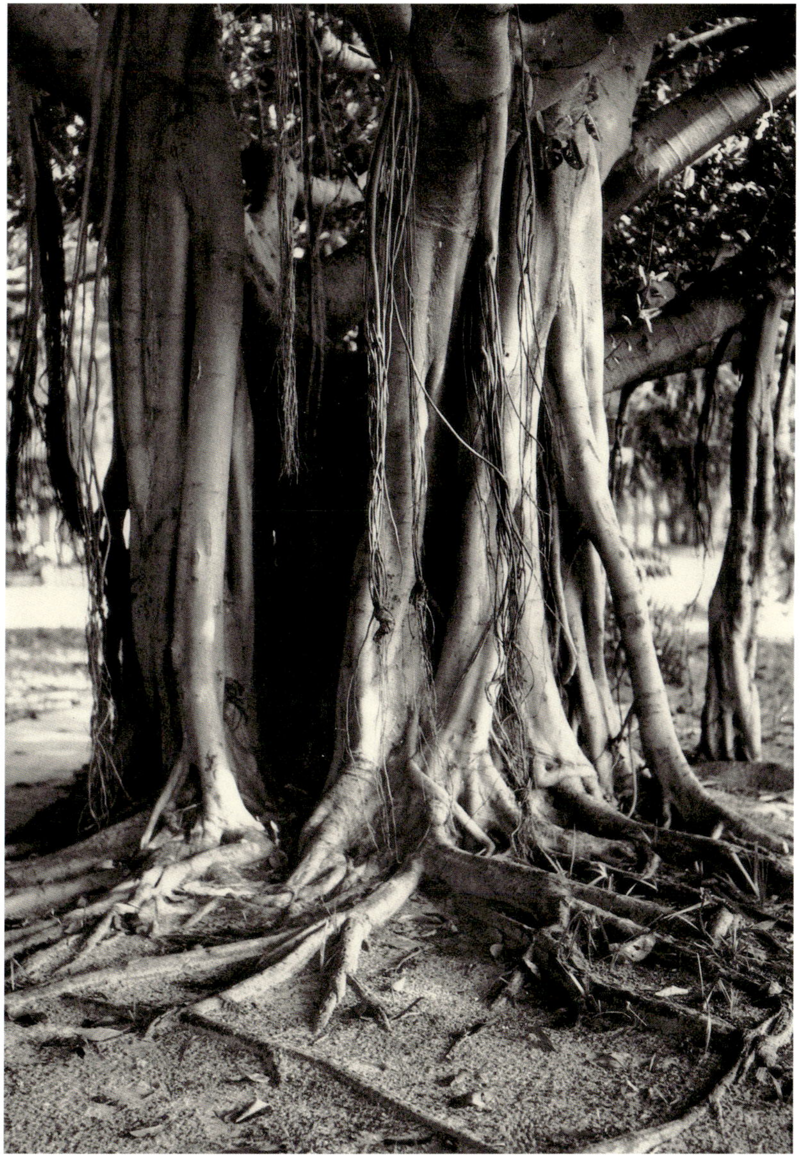

LEFT
Banyan Tree

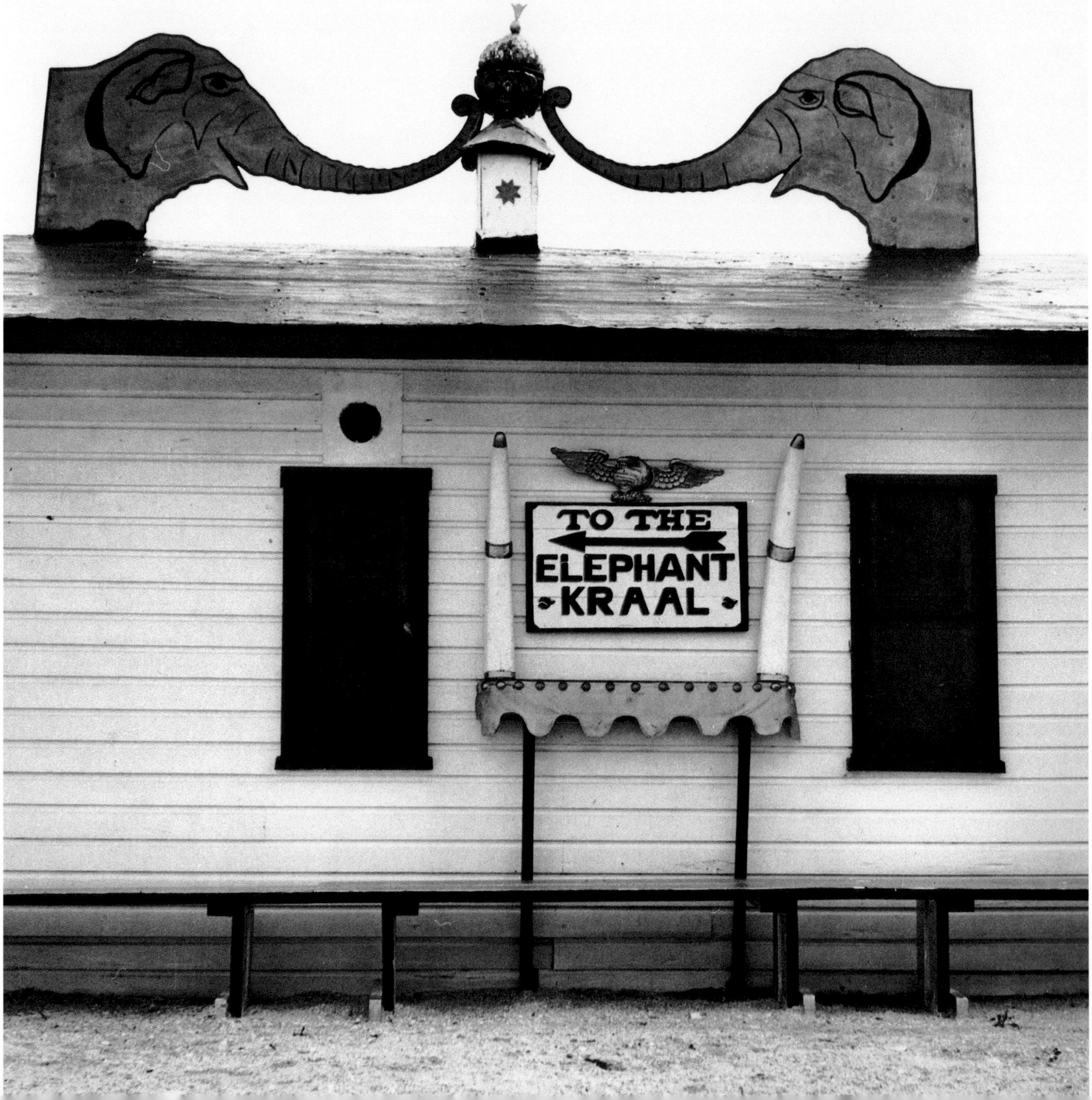

winter chill or to recover from the illnesses that plagued his later life. But there is no record that he kept up with the Bickels or that he participated in the life of Sarasota. It would have been out of character if he had.

The Bickel house still stands, suddenly back in the news as Sarasota's latest controversy. There are plans to demolish it—it has been derelict and abandoned for over twenty years—in order to widen the street in preparation for a new Ritz Carlton Hotel, an eerie echo of John Ringling's earlier dream. The historical preservationists are up in arms as usual, but everyone suspects they will lose on this one, too. The city has already destroyed most of its past, usually after great civic debate and agonizing feelings of guilt.

But Sarasota remains a very lucky town. Over and over it has been touched by genius. First there was Ringling and the circus. Then came John D. MacDonald, the mystery novelist. For thirty years he lived and wrote here, elevating the lowly mystery novel to art as he explored the moral dilemmas of that odd new culture, the Sun Belt.

And now we have these extraordinary photographs by Walker Evans, powerful evidence—Harriet Beecher Stowe notwithstanding—that not everyone returns from Florida "intensely disappointed, and even disgusted." They present a Florida that doesn't exist anymore, and what a strange place it must have been, so foreign looking, so handmade. If they show anything, it is that artificiality is many layers deep. And what better way to illustrate this than with pictures of a small town in Florida where the circus is king, pelicans fill the air, and the people live in little tin houses that they can move from place to place?

OPPOSITE
Circus Building, Winter Quarters, Sarasota

The Photographs

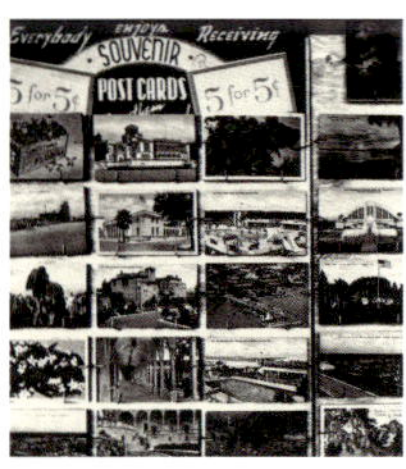

Postcard Display
1941
$6\frac{7}{16} \times 5\frac{1}{4}$ in.
84.XM.956.874

PAGE ii

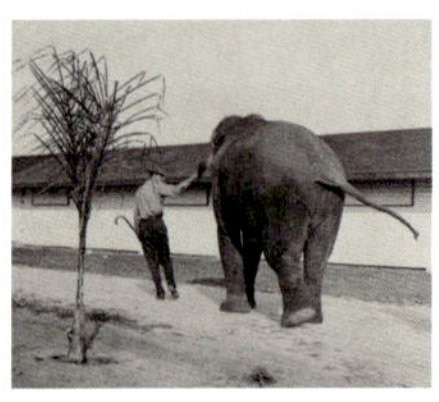

Circus Trainer Leading Elephant, Winter Quarters, Sarasota
1941
$6\frac{9}{16} \times 7\frac{15}{32}$ in.
84.XM.956.941

PAGE iii

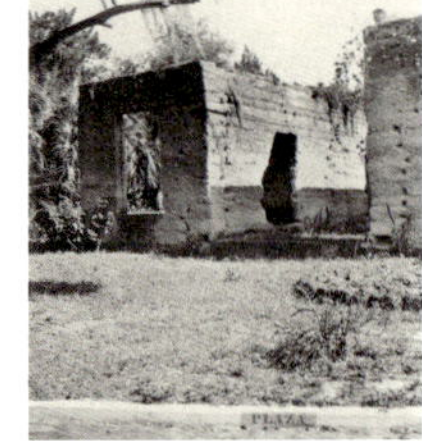

Ruin Tabby Construction
1941
$7\frac{11}{16} \times 6\frac{7}{16}$ in.
84.XM.956.844

PAGE iv

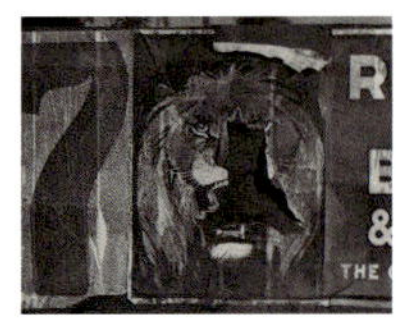

Torn Ringling Brothers Poster
1941
$6\frac{17}{32} \times 8\frac{1}{16}$ in.
84.XM.956.914

PAGE v

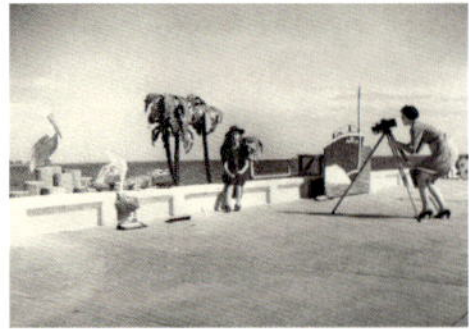

Resort Photographer at Work
1941
$6\frac{1}{4} \times 8\frac{13}{16}$ in.
84.XM.956.948

PAGE ix

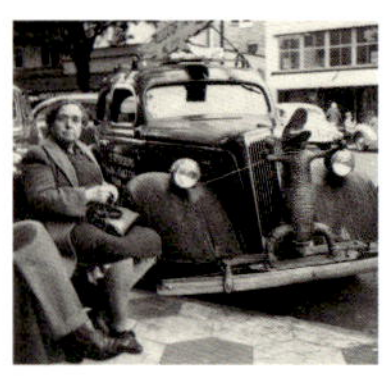

Woman with Car from "St. Petersburg Alligator Farm"
1941
$5\frac{11}{16} \times 5\frac{1}{2}$ in.
84.XM.956.938

PAGE x

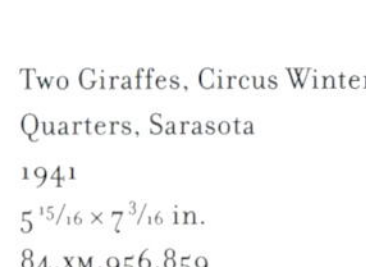

Two Giraffes, Circus Winter Quarters, Sarasota
1941
$5\frac{15}{16} \times 7\frac{3}{16}$ in.
84.XM.956.859

PAGE xii

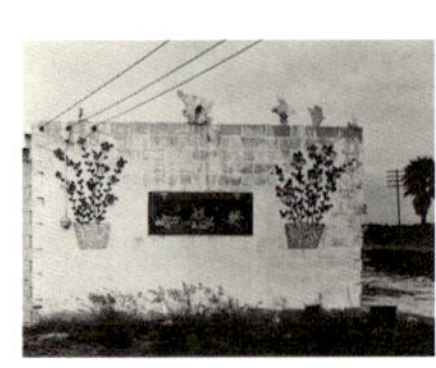

Concrete Block Building with Shell Decoration
1941
$7 \times 8\frac{31}{32}$ in.
84.XM.956.871

PAGE 3

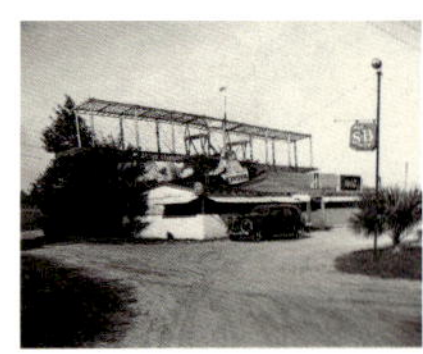

Mystery Ship Roadside Bar
1941
$6\frac{9}{16} \times 7\frac{31}{32}$ in.
84.XM.956.936

PAGE 4

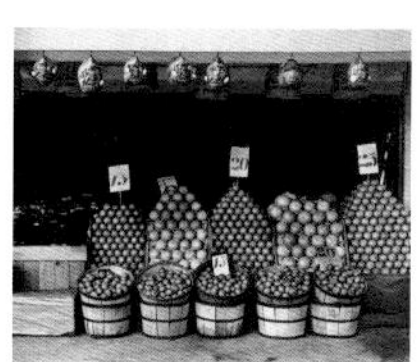

Souvenir Shop Display
1941
$6\frac{29}{32} \times 8$ in.
84.XM.956.935
PAGE 6

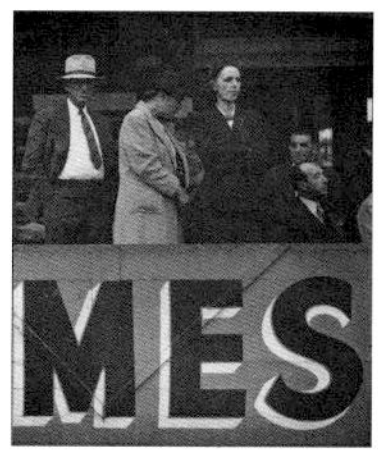

Racetrack Spectators
1941
$8\frac{25}{32} \times 7\frac{3}{16}$ in.
84.XM.956.1076
PAGE 7

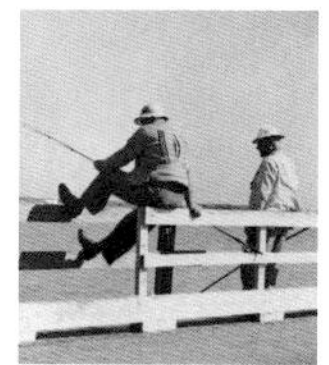

Two Men Fishing
1941
$5\frac{9}{16} \times 4\frac{21}{32}$ in.
84.XM.956.908
PAGE 10

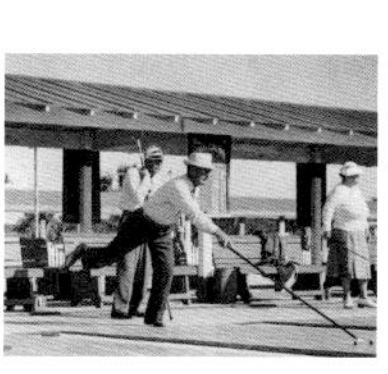

Shuffleboard Players
1941
$5\frac{5}{32} \times 7\frac{23}{32}$ in.
84.XM.956.913
PAGE 11

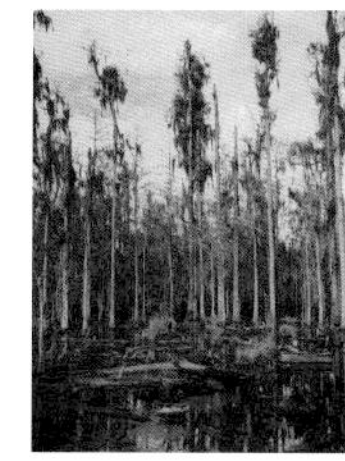

Cypress Swamp
1941
$9 \times 6\frac{5}{8}$ in.
84.XM.956.879
PAGE 13

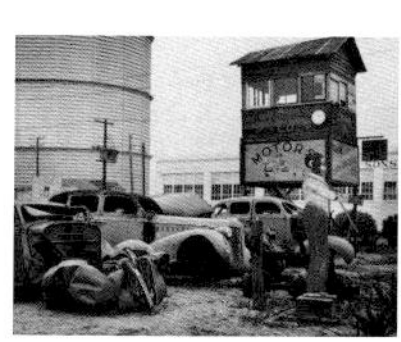

Auto Graveyard at Tampa
1941
$15\frac{11}{16} \times 7\frac{3}{16}$ in.
84.XM.956.944
PAGE 14

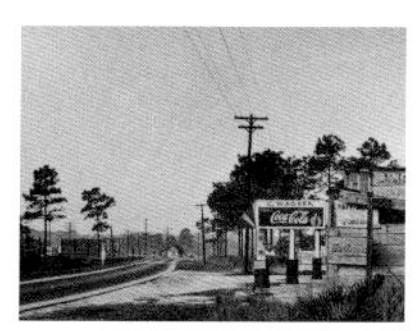

Upstate Roadside Landscape
1941
$5\frac{1}{16} \times 6\frac{15}{32}$ in.
84.XM.956.937
PAGE 15

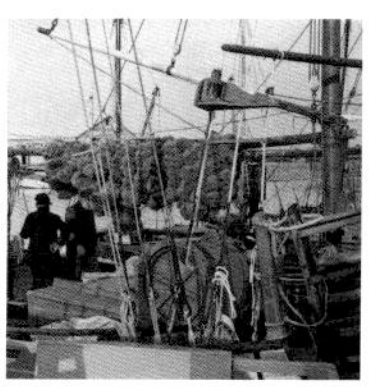

Fisherman in Sponge Boat, Tarpon Springs
1941
$6\frac{21}{32} \times 6\frac{3}{16}$ in.
84.XM.956.855
PAGE 16

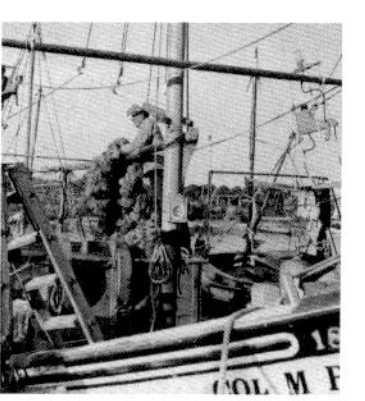

Sponge-Diver's Boat, Tarpon Springs
1941
$6\frac{3}{8} \times 6\frac{7}{32}$ in.
84.XM.956.929
PAGE 17

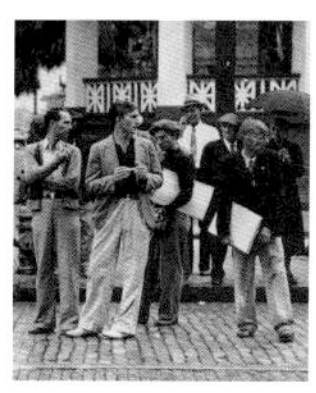

Crowd Waiting at Street Corner, Tampa
1941
$5\frac{5}{8} \times 4\frac{19}{32}$ in.
84.XM.956.246
PAGE 19

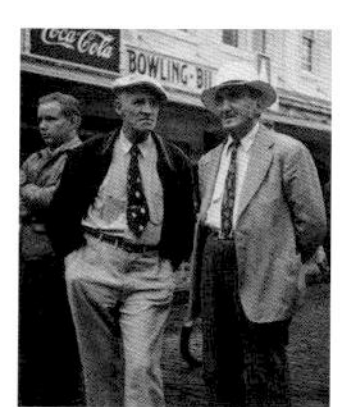

Men in the Street at Tampa
1941
$6\frac{1}{8} \times 4\frac{15}{16}$ in.
84.XM.956.934
PAGE 20

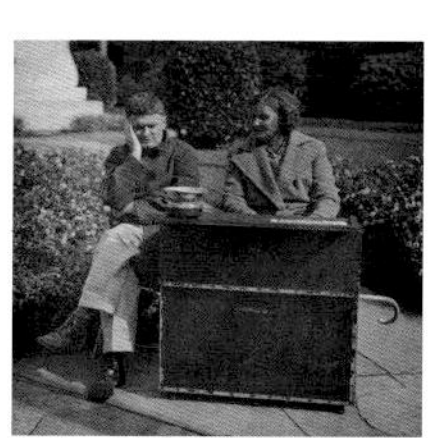

Blind Couple in Tampa City Square Hall
1941
$7\frac{1}{16} \times 7\frac{1}{4}$ in.
84.XM.956.814
PAGE 21

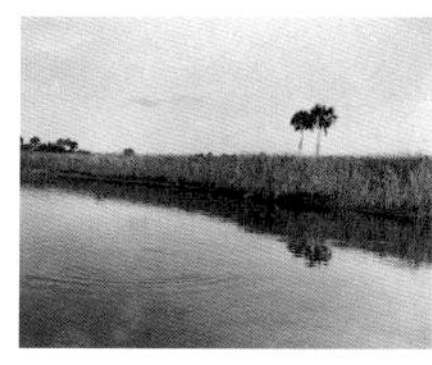

Coastal Landscape with Palms
1941
$7\frac{5}{8} \times 9\frac{9}{16}$ in.
84.XM.956.919
PAGE 22

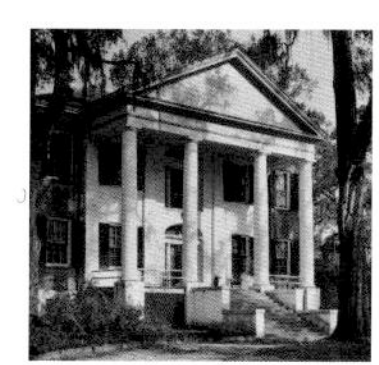

Antebellum Plantation House at Tallahassee
1941
$6\frac{3}{16} \times 6\frac{13}{32}$ in.
84.XM.956.923
PAGE 24

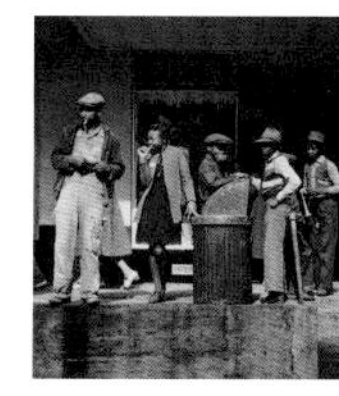

Negroes at Tallahassee
1941
$6\frac{15}{16} \times 6$ in.
84.XM.956.882
PAGE 25

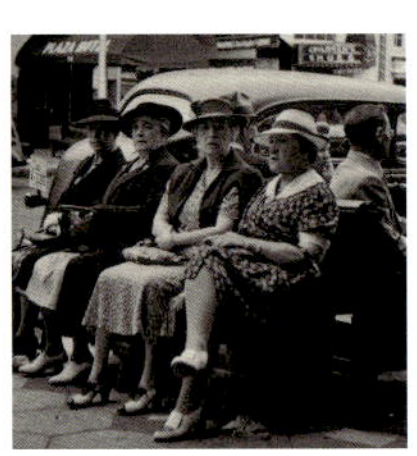

The Green Benches at
St. Petersburg
1941
$7\,^{5}/_{16} \times 6\,^{31}/_{32}$ in.
84.XM.956.930
PAGE 26

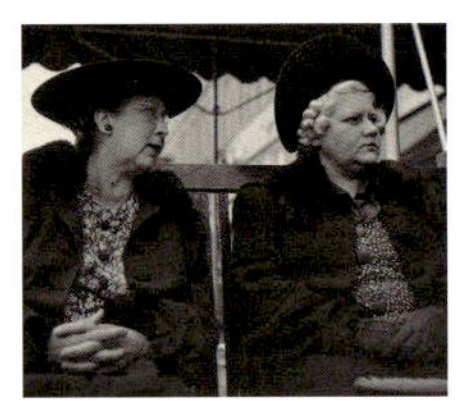

Winter Resorters
1941
$6\,^{5}/_{8} \times 7\,^{19}/_{32}$ in.
84.XM.956.939
PAGE 27

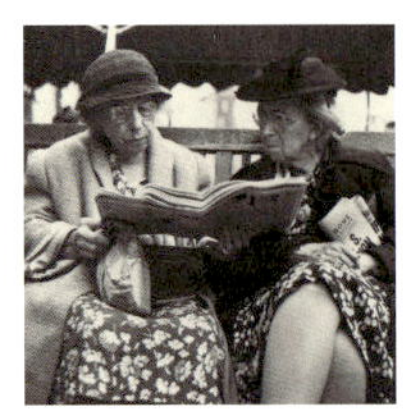

Winter Resorters
1941
$7\,^{3}/_{16} \times 7\,^{1}/_{8}$ in.
84.XM.956.839
PAGE 28

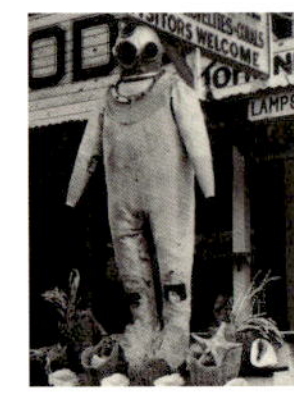

Sponge Diver's Suit,
Tarpon Springs
1941
$8\,^{9}/_{16} \times 6\,^{1}/_{4}$ in.
84.XM.956.868
PAGE 29

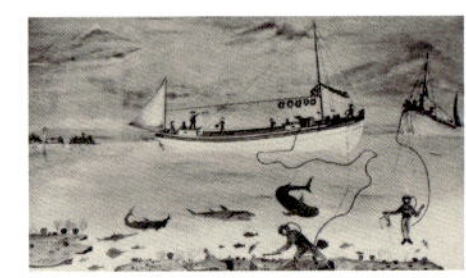

Descriptive Painting
by a Sponge Diver
1941
$4\,^{7}/_{16} \times 7\,^{9}/_{16}$ in.
84.XM.956.873
PAGES 30–31

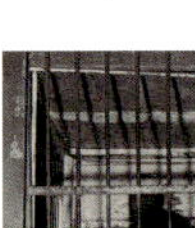

Caged Baboon,
Circus Winter Quarters
1941
$6\,^{29}/_{32} \times 5\,^{5}/_{16}$ in.
84.XM.956.885
PAGE 32

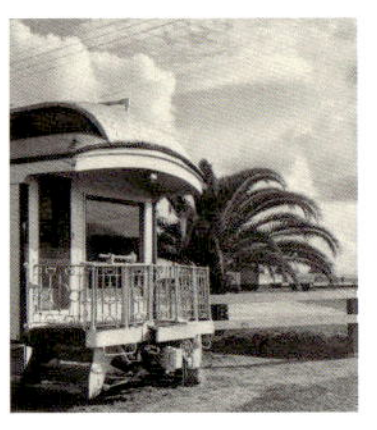

Balcony Car, Circus Train,
Winter Quarters, Sarasota
1941
$7\,^{5}/_{8} \times 6\,^{11}/_{16}$ in.
84.XM.956.946
PAGE 34

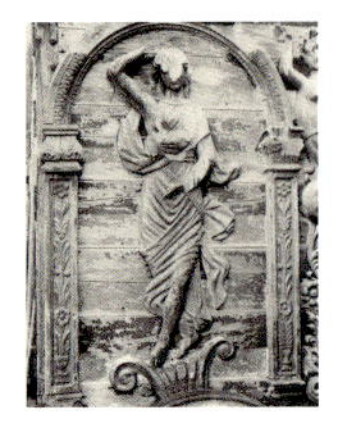

Ringling Bandwagon,
Circus Winter Quarters, Sarasota
1941
$8\,^{3}/_{8} \times 6\,^{1}/_{2}$ in.
84.XM.956.875
PAGE 35

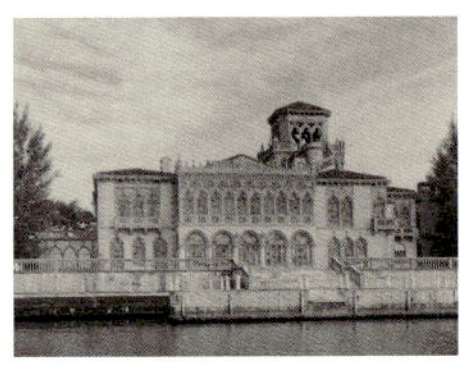

Uninhabited Seaside Residence in
Sarasota (Ca'd'Zan, formerly the
Ringling Residence)
1941
$6\,^{7}/_{8} \times 8\,^{7}/_{8}$ in.
84.XM.956.827
PAGES 36–37

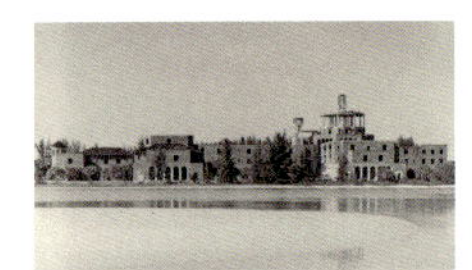

Unfinished Boomtime Hotel
1941
$4\,^{13}/_{32} \times 7\,^{5}/_{16}$ in.
84.XM.956.867
PAGE 38

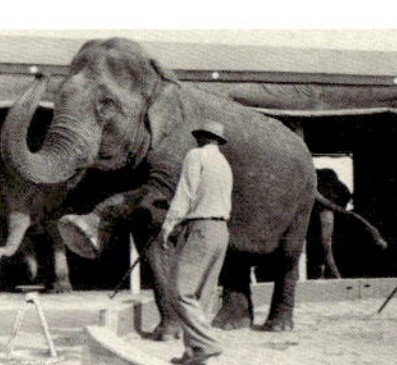

Circus Trainer with
Performing Elephant,
Winter Quarters, Sarasota
1941
$6\,^{11}/_{16} \times 8$ in.
84.XM.956.829
PAGE 39

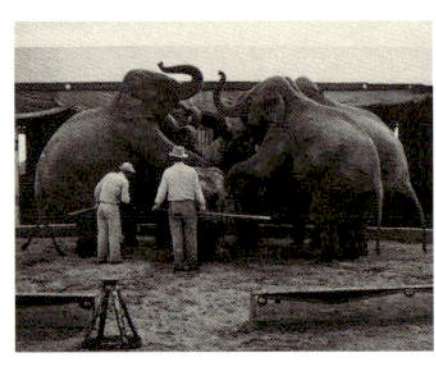

Two Circus Trainers
with Performing Elephants,
Winter Quarters, Sarasota
1941
$6\,^{11}/_{16} \times 8\,^{17}/_{32}$ in.
84.XM.956.853
PAGE 40

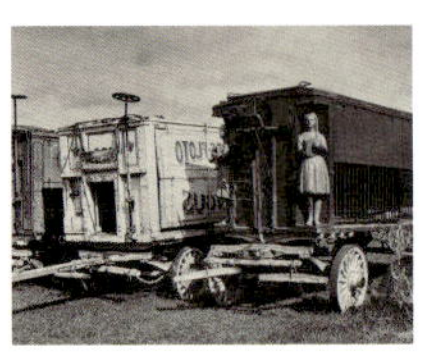

Three Circus Train Cars,
Winter Quarters, Sarasota
(reversed printing)
1941
$7\,^{3}/_{16} \times 8\,^{15}/_{16}$ in.
84.XM.956.803
PAGE 42

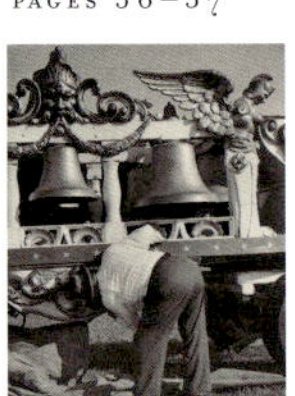

Man at Work on Circus Wagon,
Sarasota
1941
$8\,^{23}/_{32} \times 6\,^{23}/_{32}$ in.
84.XM.956.940
PAGE 43

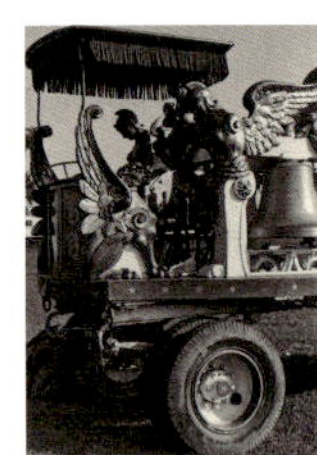

Detail of Circus Wagon, Sarasota
1941
$8\,^{3}/_{4} \times 5\,^{15}/_{16}$ in.
84.XM.956.877
PAGE 44

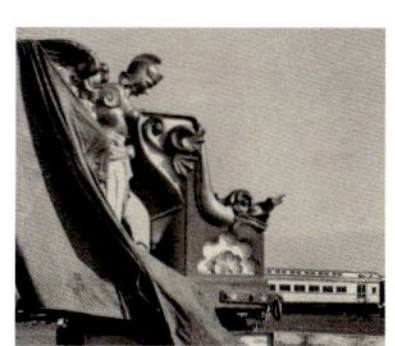

Circus Winter Quarters, Sarasota
1941
7 3/16 × 8 7/32 in.
84.XM.956.942
PAGE 45

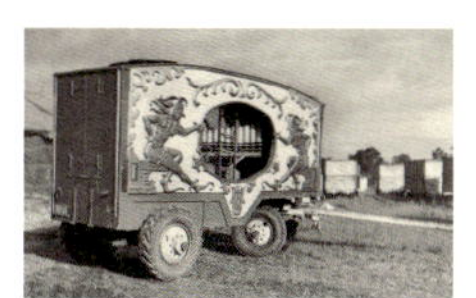

Circus Wagon (Calliope Car), Winter Quarters, Sarasota
1941
5 13/16 × 9 1/8 in.
84.XM.956.851
PAGE 46

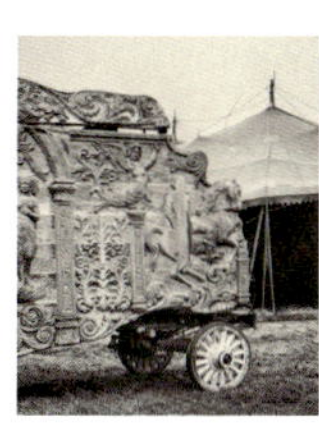

Ringling Bandwagon, Circus Winter Quarters, Sarasota
1941
7 11/16 × 6 29/32 in.
84.XM.956.831
PAGE 47

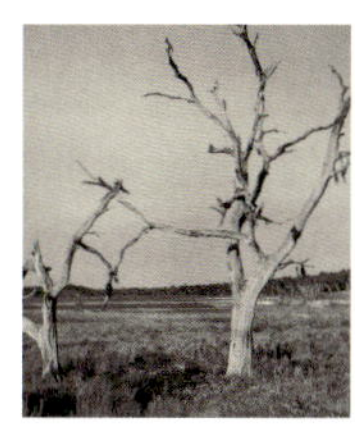

Inland Landscape
1941
7 15/32 × 6 3/16 in.
84.XM.956.837
PAGE 49 LEFT

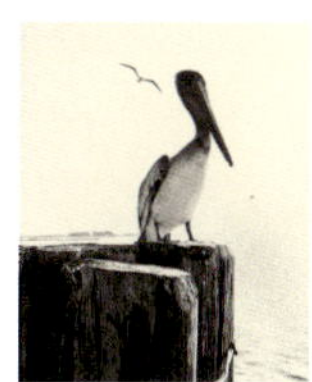

Pelican on a Dock
1941
8 × 6 7/16 in.
84.XM.956.876
PAGE 49 RIGHT

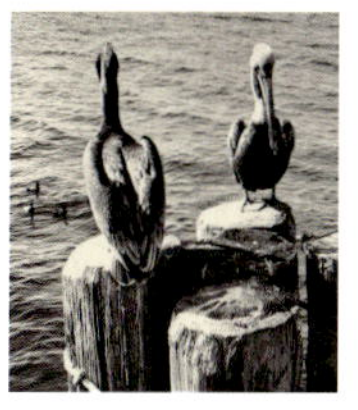

Two Pelicans on a Dock
1941
6 19/32 × 5 11/16 in.
84.XM.956.925
PAGE 51

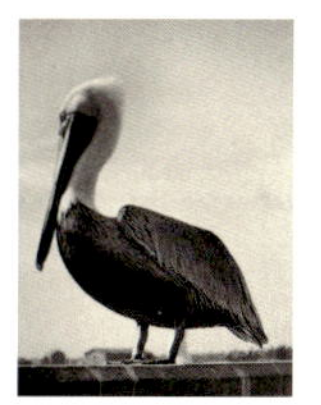

Pelican
1941
7 1/4 × 5 1/4 in.
84.XM.956.860
PAGE 52

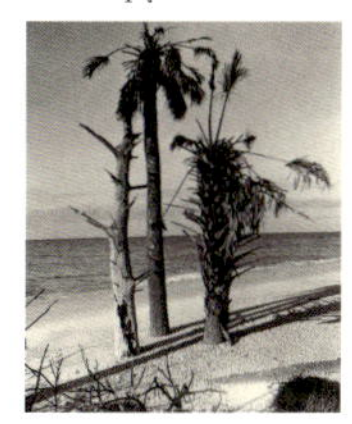

Three Palms
1941
8 1/32 × 6 1/2 in.
84.XM.956.816
PAGE 53 LEFT

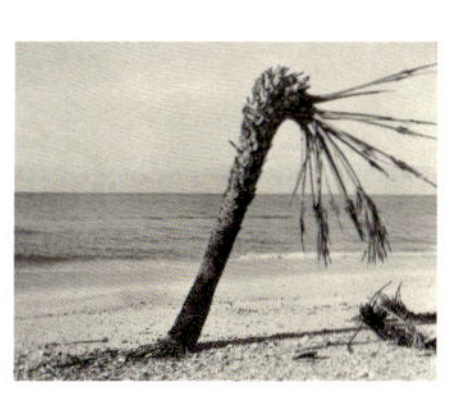

Gulf of Mexico
1941
5 15/16 × 7 7/16 in.
84.XM.956.931
PAGE 53 RIGHT

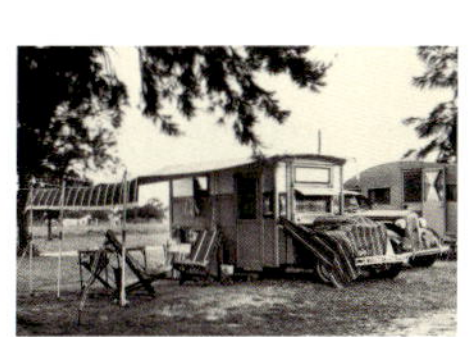

Recreational Vehicle with Striped Canopy
1941
5 3/4 × 8 11/16 in.
84.XM.956.932
PAGES 54–55

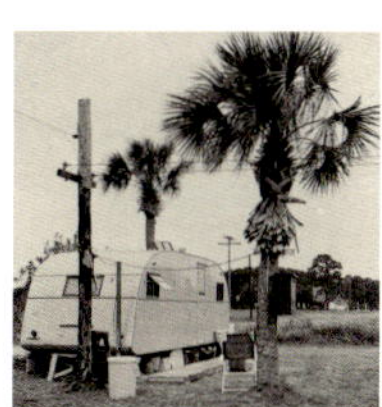

Trailer in Camp, Sarasota
1941
6 31/32 × 6 13/32 in.
84.XM.956.945
PAGE 56

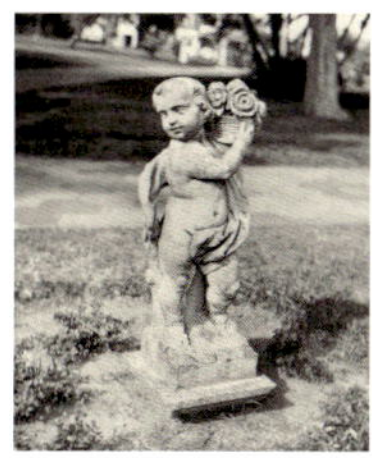

Statuette of a Cherub
1941
8 7/8 × 7 1/16 in.
84.XM.956.920
PAGE 58

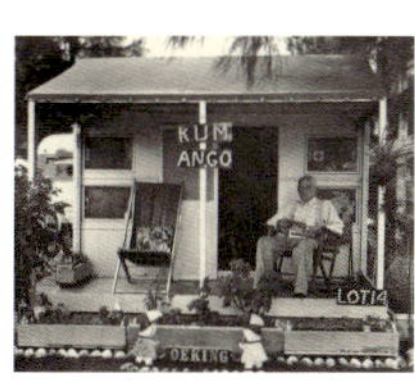

Municipal Trailer Camp
1941
6 1/32 × 7 3/32 in.
84.XM.956.798
PAGE 59

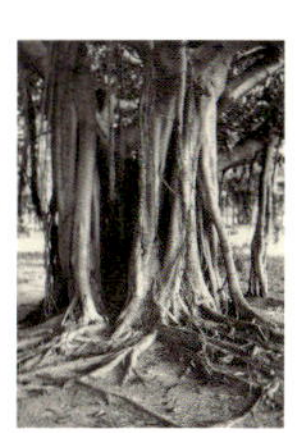

Banyan Tree
1941
7 9/16 × 5 5/16 in.
84.XM.956.943
PAGE 61

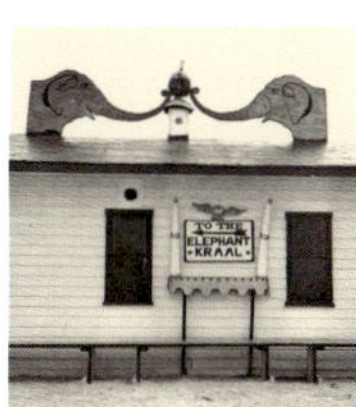

Circus Building, Winter Quarters, Sarasota
1941
6 25/32 × 6 5/32 in.
84.XM.956.883
PAGE 62

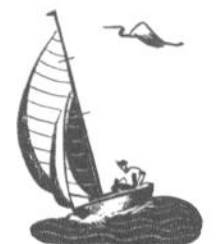

Library of Congress
Cataloging-in-Publication Data

Evans, Walker, 1903–1975.
Walker Evans: Florida / with an essay by Robert Plunket.
p. cm.
ISBN 0-89236-566-8
1. Gulf Coast (Fla.) Pictorial works. 2. Gulf Coast (Fla.) Description and travel. 3. Florida Pictorial works. 4. Florida—Description and travel. I. Plunket, Robert. II. Title.
F317.G8E93 2000
975.9—dc21 99-27279
CIP

1200 Getty Center Drive
Suite 400
Los Angeles, California
90049-1681

www.getty.edu/publications

Publisher
Christopher Hudson
Managing Editor
Mark Greenberg

The J. Paul Getty Museum acknowledges the cooperation of The Walker Evans Archive at The Metropolitan Museum of Art.

Project Staff

Editor
John Harris
Designer
Vickie Sawyer Karten
Production Coordinator
Suzanne Petralli Meilleur
Photographers
Charles Passela
Ellen Rosenbery
Photographic Technician
Rebecca Vera-Martinez
Cataloging Assistant II, Department of Photographs
Michael Hargraves

Printed by
Gardner Lithograph
Buena Park, California

Bound by
Roswell Book Bindery
Phoenix, Arizona

Map of Florida and line art from: *Florida: A Guide to the Southernmost State* by the Federal Writers' Project of the Work Projects Administration, edited by the State of Florida. Copyright 1939 by the State of Florida Dept. of Public Instruction. Used by permission of Oxford University Press, Inc.

FRONT COVER: *Trailer in Camp, Sarasota*; see page 56.

BACK COVER: *Three Palms*; see page 53.